The Change
Managem

D1103542

C.A. C   nall
Henle   *agemei*

THOMSON
™

Australia • Canada • Mexico • Singapore • Spain • United Kingdom • United States

For more information, contact Thomson Learning, High Holborn House, 50–51 Bedford Row, London, WC1R 4LR or visit us on the World Wide Web at: http://www.thomsonlearning.co.uk

BRITISH LIBRARY
CATALOGUING-IN-PUBLICATION DATA
A catalogue record for this book is available from the British Library

ISBN 1-86152-961-9

Typeset by LaserScript, Mitcham, Surrey
Printed in Great Britain by TJ International, Padstow, Cornwall

Contents

Figures

Tables

1 The Change Management Toolkit

This book is designed as a 'toolkit' for the manager or other professional who seeks to manage change in an organizational setting. It starts from an optimistic viewpoint. Managers and organizations have experienced a lot of change in the last ten or so years. We are beginning to understand how to do it. Those who say change is difficult or almost impossible are wrong. There are 'tools' available to help us. Resistance to change is not inevitable. Failure is not the only outcome.

If you think about it many people say that change is difficult. Difficult to conceive because one must inevitably deal with people issues and an uncertain future. The more so to implement because the consequences can be difficult to predict, harder to track and can therefore create a dynamic all their own. In particular everyone claims that major change is hard because of the so called 'soft' or people issues. Is this really so? Does the reader know of any organization or institution which has not experienced change in the last decade or so? Would anyone seriously argue that we are not living in a period of rapid change? Is it not true that we are also living in an era through which dramatic changes of productivity, technology, brand, image and reputation are commonplace?

Some will say 'yes' to these questions but then question the longer term consequences. What kind of society are we creating? Do we devote enough attention to the long-term consequences of what we do? Fair enough, but that is to shift the argument. The fact is that organizations are changing more and more rapidly and are engaged in delivering higher productivity, higher levels of activity, customer satisfaction, and so on. This is not to say that all is well nor that all are successful. Rather it is to note that organizations have grown volumes, activity and profitability during a period in which ever more complex demands (for customer satisfaction and business ethics) have been added into the increasingly complex and diverse environments in which we operate. The challenge facing the senior executive is bigger and yet more change is being achieved.

Thus we must be getting something right! It may be possible to see change as demanding and tiring but not as necessarily inherently difficult. This argument partly turns on the idea of 'resistance to change'. Some argue that people are inherently resistant to change. Whether for personal or institutional reasons, strategic change can be beset by opposition from key stakeholders, whether key professionals or other vested interests, unions and the like. This is true and I do not seek to diminish the importance of this point. But it is a partial truth. Much of what we refer to as 'resistance to change' is really 'resistance to uncertainty'. Thus the resistance derives from the process of handling and managing change, not from the change as such.

If people understand what is to be achieved, why, how and by whom, this can help. If they understand the impact on themselves, even more so. This is not to argue that all resistance disappears. Indeed you can argue that more information provided to those who seek to obstruct change because their interests are threatened may help them to carry out their obstruction. But is that a matter of stakeholder handling, timing and tactics? My point is that the arguments of many behavioural scientists writing about change are overwhelmingly partial and, at least in part, misleading. Rapidly skating over the issue of what ought to be changed, much of the writing I refer to deals with employee attitudes, satisfactions, beliefs and so on. Not that this is unimportant – but it is not the whole story. Much of an employee's response to any proposal for change lies in its perceived relevance, credibility and likely success. If someone argues that something should change and presents a credible plan which I feel is likely to succeed, then I am more likely to go along.

The book is based upon a change management model that focuses on the successful implementation of change. The model is set out in Figure 1.1.

To be successful in implementing strategic changes managers need to work with five sets of concepts and tools as follows.

The Value Adding Company

New ways of organizing work which are built on concepts of customer service and value adding have been emerging. These seek adaptive arrangements because customer needs and market circumstances are changing. The new 'rules of competition' emphasize speed, flexibility and customer intimacy. Thus in changing our organization's concerns from control and predictability as the overriding considerations, we are increasingly concerned with speed, flexibility and customers.

Figure 1.1 **Change management model**

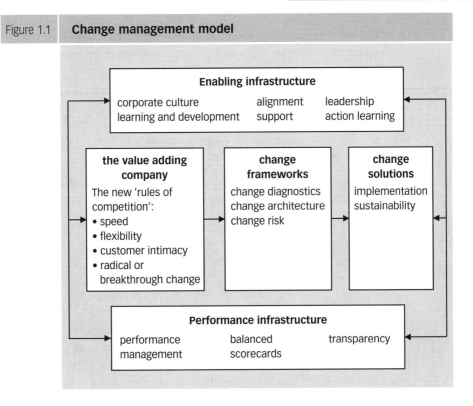

Change Frameworks

We need to understand best practice in change diagnosis. What kinds of tools and frameworks will enable us to develop valid data and thereby solutions credible to key stakeholders? How can we create authentic diagnosis? What processes should we follow?

What do we mean by change architecture? Simply stated we mean that set of arrangements, systems, resources and processes through which we engage people in 'productive reasoning' focused upon creating a new future. The principles can be applied in various ways such as strategy forums, communication cascades, 'town meetings', 'open-space events', balanced scorecards and much more. These have the following goals:

1. We seek to clarify governance and accountability for strategic change.

2. We seek to engage key stakeholders in appropriate ways.

3. We seek to secure alignment for all or at least a critical mass of key stakeholders in ways supportive of success, however defined.

4. We seek effective, credible and accessible performance measures provided on a relatively transparent basis.

5. We seek a balanced set of performance measures (i.e. covering finance, activity, quality, adaptability, markets, customer and employee satisfaction etc.) presented on a common platform.

6. We seek to acquire or develop the new skills and capabilities and to mobilize commitment and resources.

And what of change risk? What is likely to be the risk-return equation associated with a particular set of proposals? Clearly this requires analysis of two ideas. First how ambitious are the proposals? Second how ready is the organization to accept and implement major changes? Is it possible to assess this via an implementation index? It is self-evident that the more ambitious the proposals, the higher the risk, other things being equal. However, in a turnaround situation or in a situation where the organization possesses a high degree of change readiness and capability – high implementation index – it will be more complex. Here proposals of low ambition may be deemed irrelevant! Clearly these considerations are interconnected.

Ambition and Strategic Change

How then can business leaders conceive ambitious strategic change? What does ambition mean in this context? Clearly competitiveness is key. Just as clearly understanding the assets upon which competitiveness can be based is also important. But we must also beware naïve assumptions. As Hampden-Turner (1990) demonstrates, a focus on a single factor can bring immediate success and longer term failure, but Kay (1993) probably lays the more appropriate foundation. For him the differentiator upon which market power is based is known as 'distinctive capability' and is based on the following:

- reputation – essentially the market perception of product/service offerings in terms of tangible attributes linked to brands
- architecture – the relationship of resources including knowledge and flexibility, both internal and external, and the networks that the firm can draw upon
- innovation – the capacity to change.

For distinctive capabilities to be a source of competitive advantage however, they must be *sustainable*. Here the truth is that nothing is ultimately sustainable as the fortunes over time of many major corporations demonstrate all too clearly. Scale and market share help but Kay (1993) infers that the management of public policy might be just as important (Microsoft?). All of this points to the need to understand how to create and maintain value added as the foundation of corporate success, following Kay (1993) and Porter (1985).

Value-based management is a watchword of current management practices. It means different things to different observers. For some it is about economic value added, shareholder value and the like. For others the key is social capital (Fukuyama, 1995). Taking the latter view, others see value-based management as more than simply a matter of value added. Mission, purposes and strategy require or imply a statement of corporate values. Managing a business as if values matter attracts our attention: herein lies the argument about alignment. Success will come to those whose strategic architecture aligns vision, mission, values, strategy, structure etc.

A recent proponent of this view is Markides (2000) for whom sustaining advantage is achieved by:

1. Organizing the various activities of the architecture into 'tight' systems which support and reinforce each other. In essence the advantage is sustained because whilst imitators can adopt various ideas and techniques, the ability to manage interfaces really well is difficult to copy.

2. Creating an underlying organizational environment of culture, structure, incentives and people which is also difficult to copy.

Both describe alignment, but Markides goes on to argue that success often comes precisely through avoiding the tendency to copy. Instead of competing head to head with an existing set of competitors, each with well-protected positions, the key is to create a new strategic position by changing the rules of the game. Examples include Body Shop, CNN, Dell, Direct Line Insurance, Easyjet, Federal Express, IKEA and Swatch amongst others. Markides offers a useful framework for considering strategic innovation which, summarized, goes as follows:

Question the status quo and scan the environment –
for sector and your business

↓

Does this lead to a potentially new strategic position?

↓

If you adopt this position, can you find synergies with existing business?

The Kay view takes the idea of core competence as a part of strategic architecture. Grünig and Kühn (2001) develop these ideas into a clearer analytical framework. For them the evaluation of success potential for strategy (building upon Ohmae, 1987) requires the assessment of market and competitive strength at three levels:

1. market position   –   market attractiveness
                              competitive intensity
                              market share
                              growth/decline of share

2. market offers   –   scope and range
                              quality and service
                              add ons
                              price
                              speed
                              including measures relative to competitors

3. resources   –   sustainability of competitive advantage
                              (rarity, unitability, substitution)

Following through with the resource-based view of strategy these authors note that it is possible to adopt either an 'outsider-in' approach to assessing success potential (the market-based view) or an 'inside-out' approach (the resource-based view). However, they do note the latter as being the exception not the norm. Nevertheless what is interesting in their formulation is the way they track through from assessing success potential to the concept of the balanced scorecard, following Kaplan and Norton 1996, and on into the definition of implementation measures, for which they propose a two-by-two matrix, looking at motivation and knowledge and competencies in one dimension and change drivers and obstacles in the other dimension and interconnecting them. The level of ambition is connected to the degree of alignment provided for by the proposals.

Change Solutions

This leads to an outline of the whole question of implementation and the idea of an index of change readiness. But what dimensions to include in the index? In short, implementation could be defined as those processes needed for designing and organizing the process of change to be effective. So how can we judge the effectiveness of change?

Why do some change programmes succeed and some fail? Why can some companies achieve change quickly and some not at all? Why do more and more companies see leadership and culture as defining issues in success or failure? Why are we most concerned to establish the process of change properly? Why do changing organizations concern themselves about values and benchmarking? Is not the central issue for successful change that of 'reading' the environment correctly and putting in place a competitive business model? Is there not a case for saying that in many strategic changes the most important thing is to define the right business model and replicate it accurately? Are we really convinced with the 'no one best way' argument? This means that any of a range of business models can be appropriate, and therefore concern yourself mostly with the human-centred model.

Throughout my working career in the business school world I have often met this dilemma. Managers are often seen as unable or unwilling to take the human-centred view seriously. Could it be that in reality some of this is due to people arguing for the adoption of the human-centred view and not considering the 'task-centred' view seriously enough? Might there not in fact be 'one best way' – or at least only a few variants of 'one best way'? If so, getting managers to focus only on the so-called human issues is unlikely to be meaningful.

The socio-technical systems school was an early attempt to resolve this issue. It held that joint optimization was the relevant goal but then focused principally on work group organization as a prime design innovation. Any examination of outcomes from change projects based upon this concept demonstrates that the increased flexibility that arises is often a source of significantly enhanced performance. Employee satisfaction often also improves, and this leads to a further dilemma. Why do academic observers and consultants so often perceive attempts at change to be failures? Boonstra (2002) makes this very point. In the USA by far the majority of attempts to redesign business processes were judged failures. The development of new strategies 'runs aground' in 75 per cent of cases.

Research in the Netherlands indicates that 70 per cent or more of change programmes lead to 'insufficient results'.

And yet this perception surely flies in the face of evidence. Industries and sectors have been transformed in recent years. We re-engineer hospitals, government itself and the great companies of the world. Ford was very different in the year 2000 as compared with say the year 1960. Is anyone seriously arguing that the privatized British Telecommunications plc of today's world has not gone through dramatic change since privatization? Or British Airways?

Pfeffer (1998) argues the case that you can 'build profits by putting people first' as does Gratton (2000). In each case these authors cite evidence that appears to show that strategic change is regularly achieved. The literature on 'lean' or 'world class' manufacturing does much the same. However from my own experience working with organizations engaged in making major change, it is clear that many executives see the process of change as problematic. It is difficult to engage stakeholders. The human-centred approach is of value but not often used. Very little attempt is made to learn from experience and so on.

'Strategic benchmarking' has taken on a vital role in organizational diagnosis for change, adding an important idea to the concept of diagnosis. The vital point is to compare your own organization to the world's best. Thus we identify where we are, the causes of our present situation *and*, through benchmarking, we identify the potential for improvement and ideas for change. Benchmarking as a technique has evolved (at least in principle and concept) from first generation in which the focus was on benchmarking a particular product or system, through competitive benchmarking, process benchmarking, strategic benchmarking to 'global' benchmarking. Most importantly benchmarking represents a learning technique. Essentially cognitive in orientation it applies rational analysis based on comparisons to the process of diagnosis.

Similarly business process re-engineering has attracted wide attention with many adherents and cynics. Admittedly more than a technique for diagnosing what needs to be changed, it nevertheless incorporates techniques for diagnosis. Most importantly proponents of this approach conceive it as a technology for breakthrough or 'discontinuous leaps in performance'. The focus is on 'business architecture' – locations, structure, technology and skills. Alongside the analysis of the business architecture conceived in terms of value added, is risk assessment looking at change and organizations' issues. Our contention is that in techniques such as benchmarking and business process re-engineering, we see a combination of the soft organizational development approaches of the 1970s and the socio-technical systems school, now operationalized because of the opportunities provided by new information infrastructures. Thus diagnosis has become more thorough and broader in scope. In practice it may be that the potential of these approaches has been underutilized, however.

Transforming the Organization

Managing major changes successfully requires us to take an organization-wide approach. Change creates stress and strain both for those who support change (through over-work, the challenge of leading change in an uncertain world, the pressure of dealing with other, often anxious people, the inherent uncertainties, all are subject to it in some degree) and for those who are either indifferent, opposed or fearful of change.

Organizational learning is a vital component of effective change. Following the work of Quinn (see in particular Quinn, 1992) organizational restructuring and strategic change should be based on effective diagnosis and benchmarking, information and incentive systems. A key point however, in achieving strategic change amidst organizational circumstances looking less and less like traditional hierarchical structures is that 'managed incrementalism' is a strategy for change implementation explicitly designed to manage risk. However, this does not need to imply that change is slow, random or gradual.

All of this assumes that change implementation requires the following:

- an awareness of the need for change
- the case for changes is made convincingly and credibly
- change is a learning process; you don't get everything right initially
- dramatic changes can feel chaotic and uncertain as people seek to come to terms with new skills, etc.
- attention must be given to broadening and mobilizing support for change, whether through task forces and project teams, through the use of incentive systems and training, or through pilot schemes
- the vision and focus for the organization must be crystalized but not necessarily at the outset – indeed initially the vision may be very broad, much has yet to be learned before an emerging strategic vision can be articulated
- people and the process of change must be the focus.

Alexander (1985) provides a review of the implementation literature. He supports the Pressman and Wildavsky (1973) idea that 'policies are continuously transformed by implementation actions that simultaneously alter resources and objectives'. Thus strategy (or policy) and implementation interact and emerge. Alexander (1985) also notes that implementors are, or should be, concerned both with preventing failure, by avoiding the common implementation problems, and promoting success.

There are three learning modes which are of relevance to managers concerned with change:

- learning by doing – this is an internal process. We learn by experimentation, by trial and error, by pilot trials and so on
- learning by use – this is essentially learning from the external world. We learn about how to improve our own product/services by gaining feedback from customers and by competitive benchmarking. Thus we gain from customers' experience of using our products/services and through comparing ourselves with competitor organizations.
- learning from failure – which speaks for itself but to be available to us, demands that we accept that failure will happen from time to time.

Our argument is that ideas such as transformational leadership, entrepreneurship and the learning organization each embrace these ideas. Beyond this we recognize that major changes are typically implemented as major programmes organized around simple themes – 'Right First Time' for total quality programmes or 'Next Steps Programme' for major programmes of culture change.

A good current example is that of 'time-based competition'. The key idea is that the way we manage time – whether in production, in new product development, in sales and distribution – represents a powerful source of competitive advantage. This idea has spawned another, that of business process re-engineering. At the core of both is a strategy for change utilizing analytical techniques to analyse the organization seeking continuous improvements to work and information flows and to the use of time. The emphasis is upon the organization doing the work itself, utilizing its own people, empowering people at all levels to achieve change. Benchmarking is a key analytical technique utilized in such programmes, as are techniques such as 'pilots' and 'breakthrough teams'. According to Stalk and Hout (1990) breakthrough teams should be given radical goals such as reducing the time it takes to complete any project or to build a product by half in order that assumptions will be challenged. Bottlenecks, breakdowns, failures, unmet customer needs all become opportunities to learn. All of this implies radical new ways of thinking about the organization.

Finally Argyris (1990) explains something of the constraints to achieving effective learning in organizations by pointing to the distinction between what he calls single-loop and double-loop learning. At the core of his explanation are two key points about professionals (managers and a growing proportion of employees are professionals or quasi-professionals of one sort or another), as follows:

- Essentially the life experience of most professionals through schooling, university and early career is characterized by success, not failure. Because they have rarely failed they have never learned how to learn from failure. Thus when things go wrong for them they become defensive, screen out criticism and put the blame on others. Ironically their ability to learn shuts down just as they need it most
- In common with our opening remarks for this book Argyris takes the view that organizations assume that learning is a problem of motivation. This creates the right structures of communication, rewards and authority and accountability designed to create motivated and committed employees, and learning and development will follow. Sadly Argyris tells us, this is fatally flawed. People learn through how they think, through the cognitive rules or reasoning they use to design and implement their action.

For Argyris organizations can learn how to encourage learning, how to resolve these learning dilemmas. At the root of his solution is to find ways of constructively questioning the rationale or reasoning behind someone's actions.

The BBC

Case Study

This case study outlines what was a radical change in the BBC; an initiative known as 'Producer Choice' which was implemented in the 1990s. For us it is of interest because

1 It was a logical extension of various resource utilization studies and change programmes which began to be implemented in the late 1980s.
2. The change was based upon an explicit theoretical model (Burke and Litwin, 1992).
3. We are able to assess the changes in terms of change architecture.

'Producer Choice' was adopted in Spring 1993 and represented a radical shift of culture and ways of working. Prior to 'Producer Choice' all budgets were held centrally and delegated to departments. Programme makers did not have budgets, rather they accessed resources with which to make programmes. The underlying idea therefore was to assign budgets to programme makers and allow them to utilize outside resources – not least this was intended to focus attention on the true cost of programmes, on value for money and on market comparisons of efficiency, quality and so on.

Announced late in 1991, it was proposed that the period to April 1993 be devoted to preparatory work, of which much was needed. Training and development programmes would be included. A steering group was established to oversee the changes and an implementation plan comprising 107 key activities was agreed. A comprehensive communication programme was established including the formal launch attended by 170 key BBC staff. This was followed up by staff meetings, workshops, question and answer forums and the distribution of a 'Producer Choice' brochure.

A series of one- and two-day courses were implemented over the 18 months up to Spring 1993 involving 1800 staff from different levels. In parallel, workshops were arranged for all levels of BBC staff to discuss and debate 'Producer Choice', not least to continue the process of awareness raising.

Also in parallel with these activities an overhead review, a resource utilization review and a market testing process were under way. Headcount was reduced by 19 per cent between 1990 and 1993.

'Producer Choice' commenced with a pilot period. This opened with groups of BBC senior managers attending workshops in which a custom designed simulation of the BBC under 'Producer Choice' was used as a vehicle for 'piloting' the model. Seventy-two senior managers were involved.

There were a myriad of implementation problems associated with this change, many of which were predicted by the pilot exercise. Many junior staff noted that to create 481 new business units under the new regime was to create a large 'paper chase'. Nevertheless by 1994 survey and other data suggests that value for money had improved and, moreover, the BBC now had credible measures of its market performance. The number of business units had been reduced to 200. Whilst not ever anything but controversial, 'Producer Choice' appears to have been part of a process of culture change needed by the BBC as it moved into the era of global competition for media and the digital age. But results from staff surveys, based on the Burke-Litwin model (Burke and Litwin, 1992) undertaken

Case Study

in 1994 and 1995 suggests that whilst staff were not opposed to the ideas of 'Producer Choice', they believed the pace of change was outrunning the ability of management to create the infrastructure needed to deploy the new ways of working. While issues of resistance to change, commitment, stress and anxiety were all too apparent, a crucial question was related to infrastructure. Would it be in place? If not the new approach would not work. If so staff would prefer the old, comfortable ways. If 'yes', then given the tools, they felt able to work in new ways. On this view success in change is about whether people involved see a change architecture which looks able to deliver that infrastructure, and resistance to change is as much about resistance to half-hearted changes which look likely to fail, not resistance to change as such (Felix, 2000).

Source: Felix (2000)

2 The New Competitive Rules

The global business environment is changing faster than ever. We are living in an era where businesses constantly need to reshape their ideas merely to survive. But to achieve sustained success it is not sufficient merely to manage existing operations better: businesses need to do things radically different to secure an advantage over their competitors. Thus, in the future, we shall need to focus not on re-engineering processes but on re-engineering markets, not on restructuring the organization but on transforming it.

If you recognize one or more of the following pressures increasingly making an impact on your organization, then the need for radical transformation could be just around the corner:

- transition from growth to maturity in developed economies, leading to overcapacity, more competition and fewer larger players
- need to compete against global leaders, even in once secure local markets
- challenge of managing a shift from a wide competence/local market focus to a narrow competence/international market focus
- entry of small aggressive competitors into niche segments, using these as a springboard to challenge the leaders
- shift from integration (ownership or control of all elements of the value chain) to specialization (leveraging capability in one key element of the value chain)
- shift in power or added value from one player to another in the value chain – from manufacturers to distributors or suppliers or vice versa
- need to cope with and exploit the increasing speed of business processes, in particular time to market for innovative new products and services.

These are critical issues for competitive organizations. Business transformation is a philosophy that challenges established practices and boundaries in a fundamental way. It involves challenging 'the rules of the game'.

Changing the 'Rules of the Game'

'We've restructured, we've delayered, we've got close to our customers, we've achieved zero fault manufacturing and service capability. Now what do we do for an encore?' Questions like this indicate that 'business as usual plus' is no longer an adequate means of achieving sustained competitive success. In future, this will go increasingly to organizations that are able to achieve radical change either internally or externally or more probably, both. *This is the central idea of the business transformation philosophy.* This approach to competitive strategy is based on five key propositions:

1. Discontinuity in the market is more likely to result from radical rather than incremental change, and this is likely to be driven as much by companies themselves as by social and economic factors.

2. Coping with strategic change needs to move from an emphasis on forecasting to creating an organization which can respond to change fast.

3. Approaches to gaining and sustaining competitive advantage need to shift from erecting barriers (vertical integration, proprietary technology, piling up fixed costs to create scale etc.) to overcoming or ignoring barriers (through outsourcing, building strategic alliances, and the aggressive elimination of fixed costs).

4. The basis of strategic thinking, therefore, needs to shift from an 'as is now' perspective of market attractiveness and competitive capability to changing the rules of the game, thus destabilizing entrenched players.

5. The role of leadership in this context is to affirm that 'it's achievable' (provider of a business vision), rather than 'it's impossible' (controller/ naysayer).

By changing the rules of the game, a business may be able to wrong-foot the opposition to such an extent that they may never recover: this can be achieved by driving radical changes internally or externally. The competitive breakthroughs of the future are likely to go to businesses which can transform either their market or their organization, or both. This will involve radical rather than incremental change and needs vision and leadership to bring it about. But before business transformation can realistically be contemplated, a sound strategic base must be formulated upon which subsequent actions can be built. Strategic thinking must be the foundation of any intention or attempt to change the rules of the game and the programme will commence with a searching review of this essential management skill.

The Value Added Organization

The author of the quote below works for a global telecommunications business. His company is concerned that they are not achieving the rate of change required of world class companies in that sector. I was struck by part of his diagnosis which reads as follows:

> Current change methodologies are employed within functional silos and the informal way in which strategy is cascaded through various differentiated groups and departments dilutes the value of the strategy ... (which) should be focused on understanding how the business processes deliver overall enterprise value .... Needs to develop a process for implementing strategic improvement ideas in those value streams (private communication to author, 2001).

The circumstances within which we seek to engender change are now fundamentally different. We are each of us aware of the fundamental changes going on: globalization, deregulation of markets, new technology, privatization, fundamental rethinking about the nature and role of the State, and so on. Moreover, each of us deals with the organizational consequences including downsizing, flattening of structures, empowerment, outsourcing, strategic focus, the 'lean' organization, acquisitions and mergers, joint ventures and strategic alliances, multifunctional teamworking and much more. Many now conclude that the 'mind set' with which senior managers view the world has changed in consequence.

Traditionally, we have sought to change the organization within its existing boundaries. We have not sought to ask whether or not the boundaries themselves should be changed. The one exception is a change strategy adopted throughout the twentieth century – acquisitions and mergers. It is not our purpose here to discuss this topic but to merely point out that such a change strategy involves rethinking the boundaries of the organization as pieces – companies, divisions, etc. – are added or subtracted.

This tendency to rethink the boundaries of the organization has accelerated as part of the changing mind set we referred to above, and indeed may have caused that change in the first place. Throughout most of the twentieth century the large, integrated and centralized organization was excellent at co-ordination and control and may have been good at settling conflict (although personally I doubt it albeit it may have been good at reducing the level of manifest conflict). Conversely, in order to seek higher levels of innovation, organizations first decentralized via the multidivisional form. But faced with continued problems and the inability to develop every new technology/capability internally, organizations increasingly decentralized through joint ventures, alliances and ultimately 'the virtual company'.

Here, however, they note something which is becoming a standard of management practice when the focus is upon the supply chain. Firstly, a company needs to build strong ties with its suppliers in order to secure its ability to pursue innovation, improvement and enhanced value. Secondly, a company needs to develop critical technologies internally if it is to secure its position in the value chain. Here we see the argument that strategic networks can be very effective as a means of acquiring particular capabilities and of creating high powered incentives toward improvement, change and enhanced value. Our concern here is not to evaluate the argument, but merely to emphasize the new style of thinking involved in even raising the question.

Most importantly for our present purpose we have seen a tendency to replace planned, organizational change with market induced change. Sometimes the market mechanisms are internal – and there is a long history of the development of such mechanisms – for example performance-related pay schemes, the emergence of strategic business units, the development of competence-based models for performance management, share option schemes and so on. Increasingly we see the tendency to use market mechanisms to secure change. Strategic alliances, networks, outsourcing and deregulation are all attempts to introduce or encourage market-based incentives. The idea of purchasing being separated from provision has influenced companies and governments. In the UK and elsewhere in the world, government departments have been converted to free standing agencies. The UK health service has been reorganized into large scale purchasing authorities and self-governing trusts providing hospital and other services alongside general practitioners providing primary care. Similarly, a global business such as Glaxo has reconfigured itself from having regional sales operatives supplied by regional factories to a situation in which the sales business is free to source from the best available supplier. Here the certainties of allocated budgets are replaced by the pressures, disciplines and incentives of competition.

Thus we are seeing a real questioning of the traditional way of thinking about organizations. We are seeing a move away from the vertical hierarchical model based upon 'command and control' toward a more sophisticated model combining value and leadership. Two such ways of viewing organizations are shown in Figure 2.1.

In both of these depictions the focus is upon how or whether value is added either to internal or external 'customers'.

Many now conclude that we are in the midst of a paradigm or mind set change regarding views on how to organize economic activity. New forms of organization are increasingly discussed and/or applied. Networks, virtual

| Figure 2.1 | **Depictions of organization** |

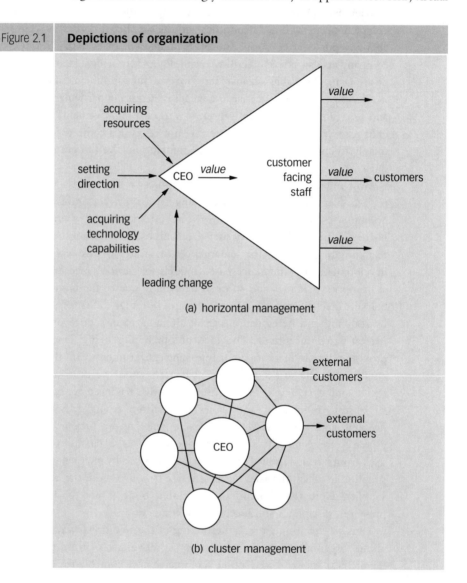

(a) horizontal management

(b) cluster management

organizations and homeworking are each variants that attract continuing attention. For our purposes there are two points to note:

1. Increasingly we see two approaches to change in use, a *planned* approach to change and a *market-based* approach. In the former we decide the direction, objectives, stages, milestones, change methods and so on. In the latter we seek to give incentive to people in pursuit of a particular direction, desired objectives, preferred patterns of behaviour, but we are less concerned about milestones etc. This is a topic to which we will return, but the basic argument is that too much attention to targets and milestones creates expectations that can lead to lesser results than could have been achieved. In the latter we establish market mechanisms as a means of incentivizing changes in behaviour. So long as we also provide adequate resources, information and support this often leads to dramatic changes in behaviour.

2. Secondly, it appears that innovations such as the virtual organization, networks, alliances or homeworking create the potential for isolation. Thus cohesion becomes a crucial issue. New forms or sources of cohesion are needed if the traditional sources of department and structure are no longer present. More generally, economists now argue that social capital is essential to success. Social capital can be seen as the extent of social cohesion and is firmly linked to a sense of social solidarity, shared values and common commitment. If these are high then we have a high level of social capital. In an increasingly fragmented organizational world, social capital becomes a crucial determinant of success.

Taking this second point further, the defining characteristics of the virtual organization are emerging as follows:

- They have a shared vision and goal and/or a common protocol of co-operation.
- They cluster activities around their core competencies.
- They work jointly in teams of core-competence groups to implement their activities throughout the value chain.
- They process and distribute information in real time throughout the value chain.
- They tend to delegate from the bottom up wherever economies of scale can be achieved or when new conditions arise.

These characteristics require and/or facilitate trust relations. This is social capital. It is interesting to note that these characteristics are also generally deemed valuable in other circumstances: mergers demand them and lean production requires them. In reality the changed focus of those concerned with organization from a vertical point of view of control and co-ordination to a horizontal point of view of value added creates the circumstances in which trust is essential to success. Fukuyama (1995) puts it thus:

> ... it is possible to argue that in the future the optimal form of industrial organization will be neither small companies nor large ones but network structures that share the advantages of scale economies while avoiding the overhead and (other) costs of large, centralised organizations. If this will in fact be the case, then societies with a high degree of social trust will have a natural advantage. Networks can save on transaction costs substantially if their members follow an informal set of rules that require little or no overhead to negotiate, adjudicate, and enforce. The moment that trust breaks down among members of a business network, relations have to be spelled out in detail...
>
> Author' note: at this point the network resembles either a market or a hierarchical organization.

In fact, managing networks, managing professional practices, managing alliances and joint ventures, managing virtual organizations and managing lean production all share these characteristics.

Quinn Mills (1991) suggests that a cluster organization makes the boxes and lines of a typical organization chart irrelevant. They are replaced by circles each representing a semi-autonomous cluster.

In essence at the heart of the structure are 16 clusters of engineers through which BPE meets client needs. The outer circle comprizes three hierarchically organized activities, namely engineering resources, business services and technology development. These units work to ensure that BPE has the necessary engineering resources, business services and technology and that it meets client needs. Thus, for example, business services seeks to fit client needs to the clusters' outputs securing an agreed programme measuring performance as the programme unfolds. Business services, therefore, acts as the account manager. The Managing Director and the three General Managers (of engineering resources, business services and technology development) form a core team. The hierarchical relationship is between that core team and the resources in the cluster. The focus of the organization is on how those resources can be configured to meet varying client needs, rather than on who is reporting to whom!

Another interesting point to note is that the role of the three 'departments' is either configuring resources to meet customer needs or

Figure 2.2   **BPE organization (modified from Quinn Mills 1991)**

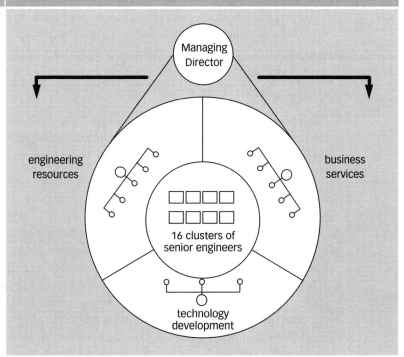

development (i.e. acquiring the right profile of engineering resources and developing the right technologies). Does this focus represent a recognition of the need to develop learning (the learning organization), intellectual capital or invisible assets? It is often suggested that intellectual capital (i.e. the intangible assets of the organization) comprise renewal and development, customer knowledge and loyalty and process knowledge. Skandia, one of Sweden's leading insurance and financial services organizations, define intellectual capital in that way. It is interesting to note the similarity of themes looking at the BP engineering situation.

Radical or Transformational Change

Jack Welch of General Electric is the business leader most frequently identified with ambitious, transformational strategy. In their book, Tichy and Sherman (1995) describe GE this way:

... The self-confidence that had characterized the company's managers began to erode. Left to pursue its course for another decade or so, this apparently healthy company might have become another Chrysler. Instead of waiting for trouble, the CEO pushed for radical change ....

And, quoting Welch directly:

Changing the culture starts with an attitude. I hope you won't think I'm being melodramatic if I say that the institution ought to stretch itself, ought to reach to the point where it almost becomes unglued. (Tichy and Sherman, 1995)

Adopting the Schumpeterian notion of 'creative destruction', breakthrough change demands new rules, quantum leaps and a radical approach to the balance between control and autonomy – emphasizing relative autonomy within a 'business engine' which demands performance.

The well known overarching rule Welch adopted sets the tone. Be number one or number two player in your sector or your business will not remain a part of GE. The revenues and margins which flow from being either number one or number two position in market share are sufficient for strategic choice. But the challenge this demands for market leadership is clear enough. The detail behind this is interesting. Behind the market leadership rule lay objectives:

- well above average real returns on investments
- distinct competitive advantage
- leverage from strengths.

So analysis underpinned the strategy. But one example illustrates the ambition.

'Work-out' was a programme of employee involvement and continuous improvement introduced in the late 1980s but the ambition lay in the scale of this activity. Tichy and Sherman (1995) again: 'By mid-1992, over 200 000 GEers – well over two thirds of the work-force – had experienced work-out. On any given day, perhaps 207 000 are participating in a related program'.

Instead of pursuing pragmatic goals, the company focused on change, process and continuous improvement, customer satisfaction and partnerships. As these authors put it, refocus from hardware to software: from seeing people and organizational development as needing to move from developing awareness of new possibilities via the development of new skills toward the development of new 'rules of the game', new ways of thinking about the business model. The interventions emerged from within rather than were applied to the organization (by outsiders). They become intensive, high risk and time-consuming. They move from working only on the cognitive level to working not simply on behaviour (a naïve misunderstanding) but on new modes of discourse, new ways of thinking about the business model. If a domestic appliances business can cut the cycle time between receipt of order and delivery by 75 per cent guaranteeing next day delivery to the customer, then new ways of thinking are evident. But GE went on to build upon the success of 'work-out', developing a 'Change Management' programme such that all GE middle managers would become 'change agents'. The former became a platform for a fundamental development focused on accelerating change.

But we still are not clear about how to assess the degree of ambition. Is there not a risk of over ambition? Clearly executives sometimes develop overly ambitions market plans. Just as clearly we may seek to handle too much change in any given situation. And yet as we have seen, you can mobilize large scale endeavour in pursuit of continuous improvement, if you get the balance of control and autonomy right. Part of the answer may be revealed in Hampden-Turner (1990).

He argues that value creation involves a configuration of values. Products have two sorts of values, unit value or market price and integral value, the value of the product to other products present or future. Here we see the GE idea of leverage. Put another way any change idea which is scaleable cannot be overly ambitious – probably an overstatement but the essential point is that scaleable changes create an accelerator effect, thus cascading enhanced value around the organization. Again with GE, work-out was scaleable in its own right but it, in turn, became a platform to accelerate change in the subsequent 'Change Management' programme. And the accelerator effect includes learning, explicitly in the GE case and elsewhere (see below). In any event it certainly involves 'rethinking' the organization and the business model.

McGrath and MacMillan (2000) talk about the need for an 'entrepreneurial mindset' for dealing with uncertainty. For them

> Uncertainty was seen as essential to the capture of profits from creating new combinations of productive resources, because profit came from perceiving an opportunity not obvious to others and then investing to capitalise on it.

They go on to observe that this generally involves the Schumpeterian idea of 'creative destruction' as new business models replace old ones. The strategists' task, they claim, was that of 'melding the best of what the older models have to tell us with the ability to rapidly sense, act, and mobilize, even under highly uncertain conditions'.

Any methodology for doing so will clearly help us with analysing the degree of ambition inherent in a given strategic change programme. What tools do they propose?

1. 'Deftness in the "project" team' as a key indicator for success – looking at the level of interpersonal confidence, confidence of the team in the capability of others, information flows (i.e. the extent to which people have the information they need, when they need it and the quality of feedback).

2. Emerging competence in terms of budgets, deadlines, costs, standards, service objectives, client satisfaction etc.

3. The potential for 'distinctive value' being delivered by the project.

4. The potential for 'distinctive operational efficiency' being delivered.

5. Leverage – reworking their terminology – the extent to which the 'project' will enable leveraging existing resources or capabilities.

6. Emergence of durable competitive advantage – a combination of two of their indices. Whilst they do not present such an index, in effect they argue for, and therefore we include, the disproportionate allocation of resources and/or talent.

Clearly the latter point is a dilemma but, just as clearly, the more ambitious the 'project' the more you could justify the disproportionate allocation of resource and talent. Some of the above (in particular 3, 4, 5 and 6) appear strongly influenced by the thinking under-pinning GE's market leadership rule (see above), and these authors tell us that one of them spent four years working with the GE work-out programme.

Martin (1995) distinguishes between processes of continuous improvement (such as Kaizen or total quality management) and what he variously calls value stream re-invention or 'enterprise engineering'. He argues that the latter strives for ten times, not ten per cent improvement. As one example he refers to a bank that had been taking 17 days to process a mortgage request which it reduced to 2 days, while it moved from handling 33 000 to 200 000 loan requests each year with reduced error rates. But there are many examples of how technology application combined with other changes has led to 'breakthrough changes' in organizations as diverse as Ford, GE, Canon, Wal-Mart, Citi-Corp, IBM, Dupont and many others.

Ultimately Martin concludes that breakthrough change can best be achieved where organizations adopt the concept of the 'learning laboratory'. He does not really define this formally but the essence of his concept is that of an enterprise in which there is 'total integration' of four knowledge sets:

- knowledge from TQM, Kaizan and other problem-solving activities
- knowledge from pilots, research, experiments and innovation
- integrated external knowledge
- integrated internal knowledge.

He also argues that radical change can be achieved by a more effective understanding of economic activities as whole systems. He argues that organizations in a supply chain are within a complex web of activities, and often consequences within such webs are counter-intuitive. Take the following example I heard from the CEO of a global logistics business. He was managing a port for his business. It landed goods from a ship from the US daily. The cost of doing so each day was £1 million. He noted that the 'dwell time' (of the landed goods remaining in port) was five days. By focusing on dwell time he was able to reduce the frequency of shipping to once per two days thus making substantial savings. When he first proposed this, there was major opposition on the ground that it would reduce customer service, but by reducing 'dwell time' he enhanced customer service directly and was able to invest some of the savings in customer service enhancement!

Arguably what we are discussing is the ability to recognize and harness discontinuities externally and internally. Gilbert and Strebel (1989) refer to the idea of 'outpacing' which they define as 'the explicit capability of a company to gain product leadership and cost leadership simultaneously'. In effect they argue that those seeking radical change cannot afford to adopt traditional one-paced strategies. Success in radical changes comes to those who can integrate approaches which traditionally have been seen as incompatible. This is likely to result in a change which outpaces competitors – this changing the 'rules of the game' in the industry or sector. Their observation of 100 companies identified common capabilities for successful organizations as follows:

- ability to innovate
- ability to configure and deliver a competitive offering

- ability to do so at a competitive price
- ability to perform these moves simultaneously.

They illustrate this with the case of Nintendo. Through the ability to develop and deliver hand-held electronic games they became the largest toy manufacturer globally in 1988 having not been in the top ten in 1983. They explain this in terms of the ability simultaneously to develop hand-held games attractive to young people with high quality images, to drive down costs via supply arrangements and to price competitively. Similar conclusions might also be offered to explain the success of Benetton and IKEA!

The vital argument here is that to be successful radical change demands balance, integration and simultaneous actions. Ansoff and McDonnell (1985) contrast American and Japanese models of decision-making noting that Japanese managers operate parallel activities, i.e. launching implementation activities before decisions are finalized and, at that time at least, American managers would not do so, thus putting more pressure on the decision process and often leading to less commitment to the decision and less effective implementation. This resonates with the conclusions of Clark (1995). For him organizations where knowledge is a premium, which operate in uncertain and complex environments, cannot be managed by planning and command and control. Rather like Rubinstein and Firstenberg (1999) they see too much planning as a real weakness. For Clark the answer is 'simultaneous, cheap explorations of multiple options' and trying not to try too hard – evolve options ground-up rather than impose them via grand strategy. For Rubinstein and Firstenberg more effort devoted to problem finding leads to less effort in problem solving later on, and more changes early mean fewer changes later on in a development cycle. Again these ideas appear to overlap with each other, but perhaps the key difference to note is that Gilbert and Strebel (1989) focus on simultaneous change in the various competence areas relevant to a business.

All of this leads one to think of time-based competition and concurrent engineering. This of course was the very stuff of a wide-ranging critique of Western manufacturing businesses during the last 20 years or so of the last millennium, see for example Clark and Fujimoto (1991) and note the themes they conclude as important for all sectors of the economy:

1. The need to achieve superior performance in product development in terms of time, productivity and quality:

- lead times a driver
- productivity a key differentiator

- total product quality and integrity, i.e. in terms of the whole system on which it sits and over its whole life.

2. Integration in the development process in terms of:

- communication
- organization
- multidisciplinary working.

3. Integrating the customer and the product:

- credible product management
- customer access and orientation
- leadership by concept.

4. Manufacturing for design, i.e. world class delivering performance.

What is this but the outpacing referred to above with the word 'integration' both internally and externally the key.

Transformational Change

The first 'toolkit' relates to what organizations need to build in the capability to handle transformational change. We identify four key areas, as follows:

1. creating a value adding structure

2. creating effective integration

3. achieving market responsiveness in pursuit of market leadership

4. ability to create a learning culture.

The toolkit idea comprises a process for developing your thinking along these lines. As an example a strategy development process is outlined below with two or three techniques included.

Ideas workshop

This concept is about accessing and organizing ideas about how to take the business forward. Typically you organize an ideas workshop, and the objective of this workshop is to brainstorm, think through and prioritize ideas about how to take the business forward. Participants are often a group of key players in the organization, perhaps mixed with some frontline people, people with real potential etc. Typically in preparation you would have accessed existing data sources within the business, e.g. sales force feedback, customer satisfaction data, and asked all employees to offer ideas, perhaps by email.

At the workshop key people would present on each segment of the business looking at current performance, key drivers for success, problems and issues and ideas for development. Participants would brainstorm, then combine their own ideas with those coming forward from the presentation and organize them, perhaps using flipcharts and post-it pads, on the matrix below.

Now we have a set of ideas organized into two dimensions, one ranging from doing more of what we currently do – business as usual plus – to radically growing the business, and the other covering building momentum in and through the current business through creating capability either to do that or to develop wholly new business lines culminating in ideas which will add significant value to the business, i.e. new products/services, new markets and channels, new business models and so on.

The next step is to understand how to assess priority, and the second matrix-based technique in Figure 2.4 can help us think about that issue.

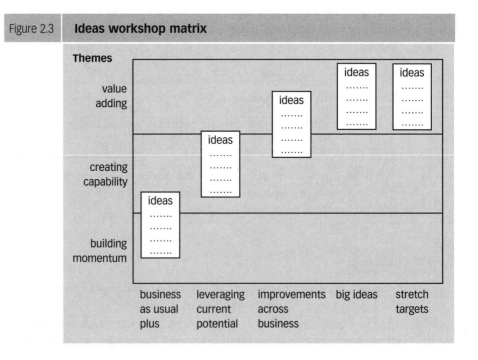

Figure 2.3 **Ideas workshop matrix**

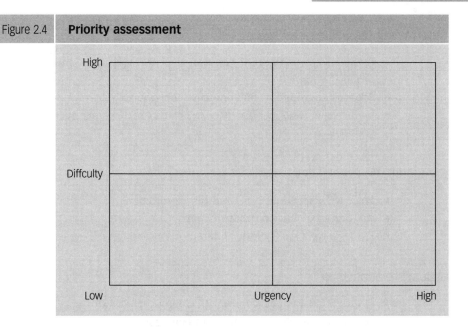

Figure 2.4 **Priority assessment**

Again using post-its we would organize the ideas into this matrix. Urgency would be linked to business benefit and/or risk management. Difficulty relates to issues of capability and change management.

Having completed these two analyses, typically a process of filtering is undertaken to consolidate ideas into key themes which task forces can work upon. We will look at how that process can be utilized in a later chapter.

Assessing strategic performance

Here is a checklist of questions to use when looking at the value your organization is adding.

Market-driven culture and learning organization

- Do we have a clear and simple process for collecting market information (customers, competitors, technology, economic and regulatory changes)?
- Do we have effective processes for capturing, sharing, interpreting and using information?
- Are we a learning organization: drawing from experience, testing new ideas, leveraging existing knowledge, open to new ideas?

Determining the value proposition

- Is there a clear strategy for creating superior customer value? Is it producing results?
- Are we committed to building customer equity?
- Is our value strategy responsive to changes in customer needs and preferences?

Competing on capabilities

- Have we mapped and analysed our capabilities?
- Are our capabilities difficult to copy?
- Do we have a strategy for building on our strengths?

Building relationships

- Do we regularly review our relationship strategies with stakeholders, i.e. customers, suppliers, partners and competitors?
- Do we have processes for evaluating and selecting relationship partners?
- Do we have programmes for developing internal relationships across the business?

Re-inventing the organization

- Do we have performance indicators to highlight when organization design is not working?
- Is our organization becoming less hierarchical, more process-oriented and networked with other organizations?
- Are changes needed in our organization design to improve competitiveness?
- Are decisions on developing capabilities and competencies based on organizational realities?

3 Diagnosing Change Toolkit

Achieving Insightful Change Diagnosis

We undertake change or organizational diagnosis in order to work up ideas on the following:

1. to set direction – vision, strategy, routes to the market, customer profiles, market positioning, business model etc.

2. to mobilize individual and group effort – engagement, access, feedback, commitment, communication

3. to identify the capabilities needed.

We seek to do so in ways which generate authentic data and informed choice. To do this we need to use tools such as interviews, questionnaires and focus groups, and we need to be aware of and make use of existing data, e.g. from performance management systems. But collecting data is one thing, using it sensibly is quite another. To do so we need to create shared meaning from the data. We do this to ensure we speak the same language as we engage in diagnosis and problem solving. The objective is authentic diagnosis. Authenticity requires the following:

- continuous and transparent process
- management of contention and conflict
- building trust and respect
- creating a sense of urgency
- engagement and alignment.

We will discuss all of this in Chapter 5 where we deal with change architecture. But authentic diagnosis also requires evidence – we must know what to measure. In this chapter we look at some simple tools for change diagnosis. Before doing so please note that as we discuss each tool in turn, we discuss its application in a company called Money Matters plc which is the case study in Chapter 4. You may wish to read this case study before proceeding.

Functional Analysis Toolkits

These tools help you to focus on an internal analysis of the organization to identify its strengths and weaknesses. This will allow you to identify the organization's capabilities and resources, how well it is exploiting them, and how effectively it is adapting to changing environmental pressures. The exercise is in three parts:

1. Functional analysis

2. Organizational diagnosis

3. Organizational improvement analysis.

In this part of the workbook you should focus on key functional elements of your organization, namely people, marketing, finance, operations/service and business/corporate development. Each section deals with one functional element and comprises a checklist of factors relating to that element. You are asked to assess the contribution to corporate objectives of each factor as a percentage. Record this figure in the Score column, and add your reasons for giving this score in the Comments column.

Factor 1, for example, concerns the relationship between employees and the enterprise regarding pay. If groups of employees feel that the pay they receive is inadequate or if there is no clear link between improved performance and pay, then we might conclude that corporate objectives are inadequately supported by the pay system. We would then enter a score of, say, 50 per cent and record the main reasons for that score in the Comments column.

Functional analysis – people issues

Factor	Score	Comments
1. design and operation of the pay system		
2. promotion and career development opportunities		
3. training and development		

Toolkit

4. effectiveness of performance appraisal and review – whether a formal system or not		
5. skills and experience of employees		
6. organization's policy regarding selection and placement of people		
7. organization's relationship with trade unions represented within the enterprise		
8. extent to which employees are motivated and encouraged to give their best performance		
9. quality of the information people have with which to do their job		
10. extent to which human resources are considered when formulating and implementing strategic decisions		
People issues average		

Functional analysis – finance

Factor	Score	Comments
1. effectiveness of budget preparation		
2. level of involvement of key staff in budget preparation		
3. degree of consistency between divisional (unit) budgets and overall organizational budgets		
4. degree of consistency between financial budgets and strategic plans		
5. effectiveness of management control		
6. utilization of management information by managers		

Toolkit

7. extent to which managers take corrective action to remedy problems		
8. extent to which information from the management information system is used to achieve improved performance		
Finance average		

Functional analysis – marketing

Toolkit

Factor	Score	Comments
1. contribution of each product/service group (or division, unit) to sales and profit. (You may wish to tackle this question separately for each group, division or unit.)		
2. market position of each product/service group: • market share • growth • maturity		
3. extent to which this organization competes effectively on: • price • quality • service • delivery		
4. quality and extent of our knowledge of competitors		
5. use of market research and its impact on product development		
Marketing average		

Functional analysis – operations/service

Factor	Score	Comments
1. level of co-operation between marketing and operations/service departments		
2. extent to which the information received from marketing, finance, etc. is useful for managing this function		
3. management understanding of long run trends in: • costs • productivity • resource utilization • technology		
4. extent to which management is able to control costs		
5. level of inventory (raw material, work-in-progress, finished goods) in relation to output, sales and cash		
6. adequacy, age and state of repair of plant, equipment and facilities		
7. flexibility of use of plant, equipment and facilities		
8. flexibility of staff		
9. level of investment (compared to the average for the industry)		
10. effectiveness of operations/planing		
Operations/service average		

Functional analysis – corporate/business development

Toolkit

Factor	Score	Comments
1. organization's investment in business development		
2. ability of the organization to respond quickly to market and competitive pressures		
3. organization's ability to exploit new products/services		
4. extent to which the organization pursues opportunities for product/ service improvement		
5. integration of development with market, operations, finance, design, etc.		
6. extent to which the organization is able to exploit outside sources for development purposes, e.g. joint ventures, universities, consultants		
Corporate/business development average		

Analysis Exercise

For each of the five areas just covered calculate the average score. Subtract this average from each individual score to give a plus or minus percentage. Negative scores reveal weaknesses and positive scores strengths. Thus for each of the five areas, a list of strengths and weaknesses can be drawn up.

The next priority is to focus on the five functional areas as a whole. Any area where the average score is above 65 per cent may be considered as a strength. Areas with an average score of less than 65 per cent should be examined. Cut-off is somewhat arbitrary – we are attempting to focus attention on priority areas where there is significant potential for improvement. You should now have three lists: weaknesses, strengths and priority areas.

Functional analysis – weaknesses, strengths and priority areas

Weaknesses

a

b

c

d

e

Strengths

a

b

c

d

e

Priority areas

a

b

c

d

e

The average 'scores' given by forty managers interviewed in the case study company, Money Matters plc discussed in Chapter 4, appear in the following completed form. The computation score minus the average score is given in brackets in the first column.

Money Matters plc – people issues scores

Factor	(Score – average score)	Score	Comments
1.	(−12.5%)	40%	No incentives operate, base salaries are too low. An incentive scheme for managers was planned, announced and then not implemented.

2.	(7.5%)	60%	Most particularly for graduate trainees, less so for locally-recruited staff but national systems open to all are in place.
3.	(−2.5%)	50%	Off-the-job training perceived to be excellent but not well organized. On-the-job training in bank systems is seen as poor.
4.	(22.5%)	75%	Performance appraisal is well developed and seen to be effective.
5.	(27.5%)	80%	Excellent but not fully utilized.
6.	(12.5%)	65%	Good.
7.	(2.5%)	55%	Good.
8.	(−17.5%)	35%	The move to achieve a 'sales culture', poor working conditions and non-competitive pay demotivate staff. Poor delegation is a key problem.
9.	(−22.5%)	30%	Too much data, not enough information.
10.	(−32.5%)	20%	Not perceived to be considered by top management who are regarded as 'exploiting the loyalty of their people'.
People issues average			**52.5%**

The people issues strengths and weaknesses are:

Strengths	Weaknesses
promotion/career development	pay system
performance appraisal	training
skills/experience of staff	motivation
selection and placement	information
company relations with trade unions	planning

The average score is less than 65 per cent therefore it rates as a priority area for improvement. Looking at the data more closely there is at least one apparent paradox. Career development/promotion is seen by these managers as a strength, yet training and development is seen as a weakness. However, it is not anywhere near the highest scoring strength. The results are compatible because these managers see a nationally operated career development/promotion system which is well supported by the performance appraisal system. After many years of only limited training a very large amount of off-the-job training, dealing with leadership skills, managerial skills and selling skills, is under way. Unfortunately the extent of that training programme puts branches under pressure because not enough replacement staff are available. Moreover, managers and staff see on-the-job training in banking techniques as not being available at branch level. One staff member commented, 'It's become acceptable to make a mistake now.'

Motivation is seen as a key weakness partly because of the pay system and partly because of poor working conditions. There was also clear evidence of inadequate delegation to staff. This creates less satisfying work for staff which, in itself, is demotivating. Poor delegation often leads to delays in responding to customers and creates more customer complaints, which the staff are the first to encounter. It also means that staff have less opportunity to develop on-the-job knowledge.

Clearly then, this short summary of part of the case study data suggests that significant improvements might be secured by examining management style, delegation and the way in which the work is arranged. Before going any further we should turn to the second technique.

Organizational Diagnosis Exercise

This questionnaire is designed to help you to determine how well your own organization works in a number of related areas.

Assess how far you agree or disagree with the following statements as they apply to you within your own department or section, using the seven-point scale and circling the appropriate number.

Organizational diagnosis – agreement scale

1 Strongly Agree	2 Agree	3 Agree Slightly	4 Neutral	5 Disagree Slightly	6 Disagree	7 Disagree Strongly

In answering the statements, try and be as honest as you can. This is not a test, and there are no right or wrong answers. The only correct answer is what you decide yourself.

1.	I understand the objectives of this organization.	1 2 3 4 5 6 7
2.	The organization of work here is effective.	1 2 3 4 5 6 7
3.	Manager will always listen to ideas.	1 2 3 4 5 6 7
4.	I am encouraged to develop my full potential.	1 2 3 4 5 6 7
5.	My immediate boss has ideas that are helpful to me and my work group.	1 2 3 4 5 6 7
6.	My immediate boss is supportive and helps me in my work.	1 2 3 4 5 6 7
7.	This organization keeps its policies and procedures relevant and up to date.	1 2 3 4 5 6 7
8.	We regularly achieve our objectives.	1 2 3 4 5 6 7
9.	The goals and objectives of this organization are clearly stated.	1 2 3 4 5 6 7
10.	Jobs and lines of authority are flexible.	1 2 3 4 5 6 7
11.	I can always talk to someone at work if I have a work-related problem.	1 2 3 4 5 6 7
12.	The salary that I receive is commensurate with the job that I perform.	1 2 3 4 5 6 7
13.	I have all the information and resources I need to do a good job.	1 2 3 4 5 6 7
14.	The management style adopted by senior management is helpful and effective.	1 2 3 4 5 6 7

15.	We constantly review our methods and introduce improvements.	1 2 3 4 5 6 7
16.	Results are attained because people are committed to them.	1 2 3 4 5 6 7
17.	I feel motivated by the work I do.	1 2 3 4 5 6 7
18.	The way in which work tasks are divided is sensible and clear.	1 2 3 4 5 6 7
19.	My relationships with other members of my work group are good.	1 2 3 4 5 6 7
20.	There are opportunities for promotion and increased responsibility in this organization.	1 2 3 4 5 6 7
21.	This organization sets realistic plans.	1 2 3 4 5 6 7
22.	Performance is regularly reviewed by my boss.	1 2 3 4 5 6 7
23.	There are occasions when I would like to be free to make changes in my job.	1 2 3 4 5 6 7
24.	People are cost conscious and seek to make the best use of resources.	1 2 3 4 5 6 7
25.	The priorities of this organization are understood by its employees.	1 2 3 4 5 6 7
26.	There is a constant search for ways of improving the way we work.	1 2 3 4 5 6 7
27.	We co-operate effectively in order to get the work done.	1 2 3 4 5 6 7
28.	Encouragement and recognition are given for all jobs and tasks in this organization.	1 2 3 4 5 6 7
29.	Departments work well together to achieve good performance.	1 2 3 4 5 6 7
30.	This organization's management team provides effective and inspiring leadership.	1 2 3 4 5 6 7
31.	This organization has the capacity to change.	1 2 3 4 5 6 7

32.	The work we do is always necessary and effective.	1 2 3 4 5 6 7
33.	In my own work area objectives are clearly stated and each person's work role clearly identified.	1 2 3 4 5 6 7
34.	The way the work structure in this organization is arranged produces general satisfaction.	1 2 3 4 5 6 7
35.	Conflicts of views are resolved by solutions which are understood and accepted.	1 2 3 4 5 6 7
36.	All individual work performance is reviewed against agreed standards.	1 2 3 4 5 6 7
37.	Other departments are helpful to my own department whenever necessary.	1 2 3 4 5 6 7
38.	My boss's management style helps me in the performance of my own work.	1 2 3 4 5 6 7
39.	Creativity and initiative are encouraged.	1 2 3 4 5 6 7
40.	People are always concerned to do a good job.	1 2 3 4 5 6 7

Analysis

Calculate the average score for all respondents on each statement. In analysing the data adopt the following three rules:

- **Rule 1** Any statement where more than 50 per cent of respondents score three or below is an identified strength for the organization.
- **Rule 2** Any statement where more than 50 per cent of respondents score four or more should be identified as an area of potential weakness for the organization. The neutral point is included because organizations in a changing and competitive world need high levels of effectiveness. Neutral responses suggest something less than that.
- **Rule 3** Any statement where more than 30 per cent score five or more should be identified as a weakness for the organization. It is worth noting that 10–15 per cent dissatisfaction is common in employee surveys. Whilst statements for which 10–15 per cent or more score five or above cannot be ignored, this rule adopts a cut-off well above that. Any weakness highlighted by Rule 3 is clearly something not to be ignored.

You now have three further lists.

Organizational diagnosis – strengths, potential weaknesses and identified weaknesses

1	Strengths
	a
	b
	c
	d
	e
2	Potential weaknesses
	a
	b
	c
	d
	e
3	Identified weaknesses
	a
	b
	c
	d
	e

Listed below are the ten statements identified as potential weaknesses by Money Matters plc in applying Rules 2 and 3 to the case study questionnaire.

4 I am encouraged to develop my full potential.

12 The salary that I receive is commensurate with the job that I perform.

18 The way in which work tasks are divided is sensible and clear.

21 This organization sets realistic plans.

28 Encouragement and recognition is given for all jobs and tasks in this organization.

30 This organization's management team provides effective and inspiring leadership.

32 The work we do is always necessary and effective.

34 The way the work structure in this organization is arranged produces general satisfaction.

35 Conflicts of views are resolved by solutions which are understood and accepted.

38 My boss's management style helps me in the performance of my own work

Two more statements emerge as weaknesses from Rule 2:

13 I have all the information and resources I need to do a good job.

17 I feel motivated by the work I do.

This powerfully supports and extends the functional analysis (see pp. 37–8). Evidently management style, support and the organization of work are key areas. Responses to questions 12, 18, 32, 34 and 17 indicate that staff do not feel the work is effectively structured, always necessary and motivating. Responses to questions 3, 28, 30, 35 and 38 suggest that staff perceive a lack of encouragement, recognition, help, leadership and satisfactory decision making from management. Could it be that the unwillingness of managers to delegate tasks to staff puts the managers under pressure – too much pressure to allow them enough time to work with staff – and demotivates staff as well? Could it be that the lack of training – historically and more recently regarding on-the-job training – is one of the reasons why managers do not delegate? Does this reinforce a risk-averse culture in which risk taking, creativity and innovation are discouraged?

The responses to questions 21 and 13 suggest that staff do not perceive realistic plans nor do they feel adequately informed or resourced. Do they see the company's future plans as being credible? What does that suggest for the prospects of implementation of changes such as the move toward a sales culture?

Now proceed to the last part of the exercise.

Organizational Improvement Exercise

For this technique you should try to identify ways of improving your organization to deal with the weaknesses you have already identified. Now complete the following questionnaire.

Organizational improvement – dealing with weaknesses

1	What are the main strengths of your department?
	a
	b
	c
	d
	e
2	What are the most important areas in which your department's performance could be improved?
	a
	b
	c
	d
	e
3	List the practical ways in which your department's performance might be improved
	a
	b
	c
	d
	e
4	How might your department improve the quality of its output/service it provides to its customers/clients?
	a
	b
	c
	d
	e
5	Do you think you are given, or have access to, enough information to do your job effectively? Please tick the appropriate box yes ▢ most of the time ▢ some of the time ▢ no ▢

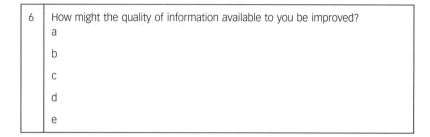

6	How might the quality of information available to you be improved?
	a
	b
	c
	d
	e

Analysis Exercise

You now combine the results of the 3 parts: functional analysis, organizational diagnosis and organizational improvement analysis.

Combined results

Toolkit

Corporate functional analysis

Strengths

a

b

c

d

e

Organizational diagnosis

Strengths

a

b

c

d

e

Improvement analysis

Strengths (question 1)

a

b

c

d

e

Blockages (question 2)

a

b

c

d

e

Improvement priorities (from functional analysis)

a

b

c

d

e

Weaknesses (from functional analysis)

a

b

c

d

e

Potential weaknesses (from organizational diagnosis)

a

b

c

d

e

Identified weaknesses (from organizational diagnosis)

a

b

Toolkit

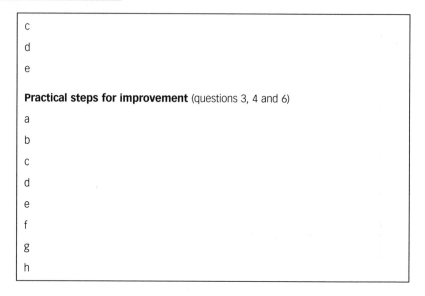

c

d

e

Practical steps for improvement (questions 3, 4 and 6)

a

b

c

d

e

f

g

h

Analysis

Identify how the improvement ideas listed could meet the problems identified through the weaknesses. In particular focus on how strengths can be utilized to deal with blockages to improvement. List possible action steps.

1

2

3

4

5

6

Case Study

Money Matters plc

An example of the analysis is now given for Money Matters plc. Listed below are the blockages to improvement identified by both managers and staff in the company.

Case Study

- Facilities: inadequate both operationally and in terms of customer service and image; inadequate computer systems
- Training: inadequate training in bank systems and procedures; lack of experienced staff at branch level
- Work pressure: understaffed; too much pressure
- Ineffective management: no leadership; poor attitudes from some managers; inefficient organization of work; too much bureaucracy
- Information: too much paper; not enough information.

The strengths identified by managers or staff are:

- loyalty and experience of staff
- team spirit at branch level
- product range
- area management team
- open management style
- customer base
- growth in the local economy.

Can any of these strengths be utilized in working with the blockages? The existing customer base in a fast-growing local economy suggests that a good platform for change exists. On management/leadership the evidence suggests that the relatively recently established area management team is seen as a strength – there are doubts about management focusing on the middle levels of the company, particularly at branch level. All staff are seen as loyal. Many are also very experienced. The point raised about lack of experience relates to younger staff who are seen as not receiving anything approaching adequate training.

These factors, considered with the earlier discussion of delegation and work organization, make it clear that one way forward would be to increase the utilization of the skills/experience of senior staff at branch level. Interestingly significant numbers of branch managers would ultimately welcome the opportunity to free themselves from some routine work to allow more time for business development. In turn this requires attention to the risk-averse culture. Again it is interesting to note that the bank's national policy of having freely available information may reinforce this culture. All managers receive all circulars, instructions, papers and so on. The bulk of information is impressive. One day's package can run to three or four inches! But once you have had it, beware of making a mistake. At area level branch managers are called in to fortnightly performance review meetings. These last all day. The area team goes through the performance data, which is printed off the computer, branch by branch. All branch managers sit through the whole meeting. Many report it as time wasting and boring. It adds to the pressure but not to business development.

Case Study

It has now been agreed that the performance review shall only take part of the day and be presented in summary form. Particular problems or successes can be discussed at an individual level. The rest of the meeting will focus on a key current issue and will take the form of a workshop. The rule will be that if we call the managers in together we wish them to work on a relevant problem. Everyone should perceive value from the time expended. In essence the changes are about structuring the use of time and shifting from performance review as a 'search for the guilty' towards a more problem-focused approach. It will take time but given the quality of the area management team and its perceived open management style, slow but steady progress can be expected.

Thus some action steps would be:

- structure the performance review meetings more effectively (area management team);
- provide more product and systems training at branch level (branch managers/senior staff supported by training manager);
- involve senior branch staff in reviewing work methods/organization at branch level.

You have now seen how to develop a fairly systematic diagnosis of what needs to be changed, identifying priorities and working toward action plans. The next step is to manage the implementation of change (see Chapter 7).

4   Money Matters plc Case Study

The change diagnostic tools set out in this chapter were used as the basis for a review of a regional group within Money Matters plc. Money Matters is a UK clearing bank offering a wide range of banking services to personal and corporate customers. Nationally the company is divided into twelve regions. Each region is divided into a number of groups and each group comprises up to twenty branch offices and other departments. Money Matters has only recently established the group structure, which is outlined in Figure 4.1.

The group chosen for review is responsible for personal accounts and small/medium-sized corporate accounts – facilities up to £500 000. Money Matters has a separate corporate division for large corporate business. All managers in the chosen group were interviewed and a questionnaire was

Figure 4.1   **The group structure of Money Matters plc**

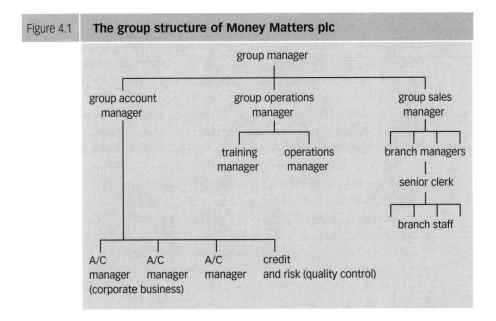

sent to all staff. At the time of the study various changes were either under way or expected/projected as follows:

- Significant development in technology including a switch to centralized processing of personal account transactions – cheques, transfers, etc.
- Rebuilding and branch refurbishment – an extensive programme is under way in the group.
- The development of a performance-related pay system linked to sales performances.
- Attempts to shift Money Matters to a sales culture.

For simplicity the following information is restricted to that obtained from a detailed review of one group: we will call it the Midvale Group. Four groups, representative of the region as a whole, were studied.

Management Views

The following is a summary and analysis of the 40 interviews conducted in the Midvale group. Before the interview these managers had completed the organizational diagnosis set out in Chapter 3 of the workbook. The interviews allowed the author to clarify their views.

Job definition

Managers felt that their jobs were increasingly well-defined, partly through the evolution of the 'group concept' and partly because of the job profile system – a well-established job description system used by Money Matters. There was evidence of flexibility between group and branch level responsibilities. Overall, however, it appeared that the present structure was not believed to be entirely conducive to Money Matters' emerging sales culture. The level and responsibilities of the sales manager were questioned. Was the level too low? Were the authorities of branch managers sufficient? Were all the branch managers adapting to their new responsibilities? The group concept was recognized as a significant organizational change, placing demands on the staff, for whom training, on-the-job experience and the process of appraisal and review are only slowly providing support. Important in all of this were the level of delegation, the allocation of work amongst the staff and the role of the senior clerks. There was clear evidence that the level of delegation is not yet consistent across the group.

Overall the potential value in the plethora of information now available was recognized. However, managers are not yet familiar enough with the information to put it to fully effective use. Moreover, some cynical views emerged. In particular, one manager referred to the available information as 'vast, duplicated, incomprehensible'. The manager is swamped. There is a need for more targeted and therefore selective information. It is interesting to note that managers had little or no information, other than impressions, on what their competitors were doing. Not all branch managers could give a clear idea of which competitor controlled the largest market share locally. (The first one-day workshop on the Management Information System was held during the final week of interviewing.)

Key success factors

Managers were asked to indicate what factors would be considered when the performance of their department or branch was being assessed and what the key success factors were for the group as a whole. Table 4.1 sets out the answers given to question 2 the tookit, p. 45. The answers were given unprompted and, as would be expected, financial issues predominate. Interestingly, customer care and staff-related criteria emerge as well.

Some managers suggested that they were unsure how the department was assessed. The process was seen by some to comprise too subjective a

Table 4.1	**Performance assessment at Midvale group**
Criterion	Frequency of response
sales volume	23
profit	22
costs	14
bad debts/quality of lending	8
customer care/complaints	7
fee income	6
staff development	6
motivation of staff	5
image of branch/bank	4
absenteeism/turnover of staff	2
good audit reports	1
dormancy	1

selection of the performance figures. Conflicting targets were imposed by sales, quality control and operations departments. More than one manager seemed concerned about the priority given to various targets. 'Is sales our salvation?' said one. Can we be successful if we 'force feed sales down customers throats' said another.

Lack of clarity in the group structure has caused a perception amongst many managers of a conflict between audit and sales. Managers recognized that there would always be a balance to strike between the intention to increase sales and the need to ensure high quality lending and control. However, managers clearly perceived contradictory 'signals' from the functional managers concerned. There appeared to be problems of communication from the group management team to branch managers in this regard. Several managers felt that there was unnecessary overlap between quality control and audit at both branch and, sometimes, at regional level. That said, managers felt that quality control was a valid function that had led to a significant reduction in bad debts. Nevertheless quality control was often unable to add anything to the notes obtained by the lending manager. This suggests that quality control should be utilized only in certain circumstances, i.e. at the request of the lending manager, for certain sizes or types of facility, as a random check, or for new business.

When asked to give the key success factors, managers mentioned different issues. Many were clear that the image and product offering of Money Matters, both locally and nationally, was important. Building team spirit was also seen as vital. Branch managers clearly wondered whether they had the right mix of skills in their own teams. One made the point that while he was now responsible for recruitment he had no training in selection interviewing. Linked to this, many managers questioned whether Money Matters was getting the right staff to deal with the increased emphasis on selling. Communication was thought to be good, although managers seemed universally to feel that there were too many meetings, they were poorly structured and sometimes boring and frustrating. Here managers were referring to all meetings which took staff or branch managers away from the branch, including training. Some managers thought the quality of staff was good and their loyalty excellent. Much more training was now being carried out, but some thought this was too much. There were problems in obtaining relief staff to cover for staff who were away training, but even greater problems for the staff attempting to absorb the training and put it into practice. Despite the increased training, several branch managers saw gaps in the technical knowledge of their staff.

Branch managers felt that there needed to be greater lending authority at branch level. Customer service and account relationships would then improve. This was currently being reviewed, but several doubted that any changes made would be sufficient. However, the group concept was seen to be working, and some managers felt that a period of stability was now needed.

Money Matters is adapting a new style in branch design developed by a leading design consultant. New style branches, new style accounts and a new style of banking generally were all seen as most important. But throughout the interviews many expressed doubts. The products were too complex. The staff were not properly trained. There was a lack of information. 'We have always been selling – it's no real change.' One is forced to conclude that many of those interviewed see change as inevitable, but also feel somewhat overwhelmed. They evince that there is lack of information, understanding and control. Most importantly, they evince powerful loyalty to the company which for some is of little help. 'Is Money Matters depending over much on the loyalty of its staff?', they say.

One interviewee was very positive about the group plan. He felt that all managers understood it. Moreover, it had been communicated to all staff. The self-esteem and confidence of staff at all levels was needed. He felt that senior managers need to spend more time in branches communicating with staff. Yet the majority of those interviewed made no mention of the group plan. This could be because the sales manager was in the process of visiting all branches to present the group plan to staff during the period of the interviews.

Customer service and the branch image got numerous mentions as key success factors. Premises needed to be inviting and staff positive in their approach to customers. A positive team effort was needed to achieve all of this. Too much job segmentation was not helpful and flexibility was needed. Some branch managers clearly felt that flexibility could be improved, albeit this was not the case in the smaller branches, as might be expected. There is nothing to stop branch managers re-allocating tasks within a branch, and some clearly do operate more flexibly than others. Lack of staff training in banking operations was one reason offered to explain why some managers operate their branches less flexibly than others. People also needed to be able to see achievable targets. Some targets were demotivating. More than one manager felt that branch managers and account managers were not active enough in pursuing/developing new business. Everyone was 'bogged down in reams of paper'. Better information, systems, premises and people might help, but one is still left with the basic fact that attitude changes are needed if the move to a sales culture is to be achieved.

Strengths, weaknesses and actions for improvement

Unprompted responses to questions concerning strengths, weaknesses and actions for improvement are set out in Table 4.2. This table and accompanying list of practical steps powerfully reinforce the analysis made thus far. Perhaps the most telling observation is that when asked to discuss the opportunities for improvement, managers referred (very properly) to streamlining of systems and training, but not to the broader changes in the company culture which are now under way. Indeed, many references to the switch to the sales culture referred to this change in negative ways: 'the staff don't sell', 'these people did not join the bank to sell', and so on. This should surprise no one. Managers and staff are being asked to embrace very profound changes, very quickly.

Table 4.2 sets out the answers given in response to questions concerning the strengths and weaknesses of the company and opportunities for improvement and constraints within the company's structure. The list gives ideas for improvement put forward by the managers. In concluding this section it is worth emphasizing that the group has important strengths and the ability to perform amidst major changes. Managers demonstrated loyalty and commitment to the company and, in the main, strong motivation to improve performance. The problems and concerns identified are only to be expected when changes are under way. There is a recognition that the progress already made can be built upon to achieve improved performance in the future.

Communication
- more open management throughout the group
- more staff meetings
- meetings with other branches and group
- meetings of senior clerks
- improved communication

Support
- improved performance feedback
- stress counselling
- more support for staff during change
- improved support for account managers

Customer service/premises
- more effective product briefing and training
- space

Table 4.2	**Strengths, weaknesses, opportunities and constraints of Midvale group**			

Strengths	Frequency of response	Weaknesses	Frequency of response
Loyalty and experience of staff	17	Quality of management calibre, selection, lack of praise to staff, co-ordination at group level of performance, distant from customers	24
Area management team	13		
Customer service, speed of response	12		
		Premises	10
Open style of management	9	Lack of delegation	9
Product range	5	Operational (split sites, local representative, high national admin. costs, complex products)	8
Branch position	5		
Team spirit	3		
Customer base	2	Poor on-the-job training	8
Growth in local economy	1	Risk-averse culture	5
		Authorities too small	5
		Image (dealing with complaints)	4
		Systems problems	2

Strengths	Frequency of response	Weaknesses	Frequency of response
Streamlining systems (returns, QC and Audit)	9	Under-staffed, resource limitations, reactive management, pressure	14
Operational improvements (service centre, technology)	4	Too much paper	7
		Change (impact on jobs, staff, 'too fast' cynicism)	6
Training courses available	2	Returns	6
		Competition	6
		Too many meetings	3
		Lack of freedom to manage	2

- premises and equipment
- counsellors/receptionists
- staff accessibility to customers
- layout of branches, open plan.

Efficiency
- streamlined systems
- standing orders system
- diary-watch system
- improved delegation to clerical staff at group office
- staff development standards
- co-ordinate training
- job rotation for branch managers
- improved market information.

The group has important strengths in its area management team, its open style of management and, in particular, its staff. However, amongst its perceived weaknesses is the quality of management. Here the focus of the managers seemed to be at middle levels of management, both at group and branch level. Lack of coordination at group level referred mostly to the co-ordination of training, meetings and returns. All led to much frustration and pressure at branch level. More important, perhaps, is the combination of a risk-averse culture with concerns over the rate of current change. Many of the managers interviewed recognized that profound changes were under way but appeared to feel that they lacked any real control over change. Several referred to the cynicism that can emerge. They felt that too many managers at all levels in Money Matters were 'rule bound'. Everyone seemed more concerned to cover their own position than take risks. This had a profound effect on the lower levels of staff. The managers interviewed clearly felt that the risk-averse culture makes it difficult to achieve changes in training and some were cynical about the prospects for change in general.

Staff Attitude Survey

The organizational diagnosis questionnaire set out in Chapter 3 of the workbook was distributed to all staff in the Midvale group, approximately 300 in all. Participation in this survey was anonymous and entirely voluntary. Staff were asked to complete the questionnaire and return it in a plain, sealed envelope to the group office, via their own branch manager. Responses were received from 208 staff members, a 60 per cent response.

The results of the survey suggest a considerable measure of weakness. Using the criteria set out in Rule 2 of the questionnaire analysis, 12 out of 40 statements reveal areas of potential weakness. Applying Rule 3 to the responses, 12 out of 40 statements reveal areas of weaknesses. One point should be made at once. The group, the region and Money Matters as a whole have been going through dramatic changes in the last few years. The organization is currently in the midst of a series of profound changes, in technology, working procedures, culture and management. In consequence many people feel, and are, under great pressure. This is reflected in these results.

Listed below are the ten statements which are identified as potential weaknesses by applying Rules 2 and 3.

4   I am encouraged to develop my full potential.

12   The salary that I receive is commensurate with the job that I perform.

18   The way in which work tasks are divided is sensible and clear.

21   This organization sets realistic plans.

28   Encouragement and recognition is given for all jobs and tasks in this organization.

30   This organization's management team provides effective and inspiring leadership.

32   The work we do is always necessary and effective.

34   The way the work structure in this organization is arranged produces general satisfaction.

35   Conflicts of view are resolved by solutions which are understood and accepted.

38   My boss's management style helps me in the performance of my own work.

Two more statements emerge as identified weaknesses from Rule 2.

13 I have all the information and resources I need to do a good job.

17 I feel motivated by the work I do.

These 12 statements deal with three key areas: management style, support, and the organization of work. Responses to statements 4, 28, 30, 35 and 38 suggest that staff perceive a lack of encouragement, recognition, help, leadership and satisfactory decision-making from management. Responses to statements 21 and 13 suggest that staff do not perceive realistic plans nor do they feel adequately informed or resourced. This raises a key question of whether staff believe the company's present position and future plans to be credible. Responses to statements 12, 18, 32, 34 and 17 indicate that staff do not feel that work is effectively structured, always necessary and always motivating.

In many respects these results suggest that there has not yet been fully effective communication from the group team to branches. Many of these weaknesses would not to be so prevalent, if the group concept were working more effectively. Allowing for the full benefit of the impact of changes on these results it must be emphasized that these data raise serious questions about how far and how fast Money Matters can achieve change without devoting more attention to managing the implementation of change with all its attendant pressures.

We turn now to the areas for improvement identified by staff. Here we deal with the questions listed in the organizational improvement analysis, and some additional questions that were included to 'tailor' that technique to meet the needs of Money Matters plc. The questionnaire asks what prevents the department or branch from being better at its function. The responses of the staff are listed in Table 4.3. Facilities, training, work pressure, ineffective management and information all feature and, of these, work pressure and facilities attract the largest number of comments. This is consistent with the earlier results. It is worth noting that staff view training as inadequate, despite the recent increased activity in this area. However, the staff are referring mainly to what they see as a lack of training in bank systems, rather than training in general.

The responses to the question of what practical steps should be taken to improve efficiency are listed in Table 4.4. The organization of work attracts a large number of responses. More autonomy at the till refers to greater scope to deal with queries and complaints. In theory this is available but it appears that in the risk-averse culture some staff feel that they are not trusted to deal with queries. Some branch managers also said that staff lacked the necessary training. It must be said that under the pressure of a queue of customers till staff are instructed to refer complaints 'up the line'. Even so some frustration is evinced over this issue. However, it should be noted that training – particularly in-branch training – and information are

Table 4.3	**What prevents the department from being better at its function?**

Response	Frequency of response

Work pressure
   Short-staffed
   Insufficient time
   Pressure
   Not enough personal attention for customers
   Others' mistakes
   Counter service inadequate
   Cost cutting
	75

Facilities
   Lack of space
   Poor facilities
   Poor premises
   Poor computers
	52

Ineffective management
   No leadership
   Poor attitude from manager
   No support
   Too much bureaucracy
   Inefficient organization of work
	33

Training
   Inadequate
   Lack of experience in branch systems and procedures
	24

Information
   Not enough information
   Too much paper
	13

also seen as important. When reviewing, management staff asked for more decisive leadership, improved support – linked mostly to in-branch training – and recognition for good work.

When asked how relationships with other departments might be improved, staff mentioned job rotation and improved teamworking as important. The two are linked of course. Job rotation would increase contact and therefore help with teamworking. Other suggestions for improving inter-departmental relationships are improved support from

Table 4.4	**What practical steps should be taken to improve department efficiency?**

Response	Frequency of response

Organization of work
  Job descriptions/clarification
  Efficient organization of workflow
  More autonomy/authority for people at till
  Delegation
  Realistic targets
  Assign people to work for which they are suited
  Motivation, payment by results
	75

Improved training
  Out-of-branch
  In-branch (22)
  Generally
	49

Information
  More product information
  Improved communication (area and region)
  Less complicated information
	48

Facilities
  Tills
  Computers
  Generally
	36

More staff	34

Management
  Leadership
  Support
  Praise for good work
	17

group/region and improved communication, e.g. quicker responses to queries. The full list of responses is given in Table 4.5.

The responses to the question of what practical steps should be taken to improve customer service included more staff and better facilities, as well as training in customer service (now under way). Information and management issues were also mentioned. The full list of responses is given in Table 4.6.

Table 4.5	**What practical steps should be taken to improve relationships between your department and other departments?**	
	Response	Frequency of response
	Better team-working	33

	Job rotation
	    Visits to other branches
	    Rotation
	    Greater contact between departments
	    More knowledge of each other's jobs
		32

	Communication	17

	Support from group/region
	    Reduce remoteness
	    Improve support on marketing
	    Co-ordination of requests for information
	    Less condescending requests for information
		14

	Organization of work
	    Greater accuracy
	    Keep relevant information together
		12

Staff were asked to rate whether or not they were given, or had access to, enough information to do their job effectively. The results are as follows:

Yes	38
Most of the time	80
Some of the time	66
No	18

The results suggest that staff are not entirely satisfied with the information available to them. When asked how information might be improved staff referred to the organization of information and to the use of meetings. Table 4.7 lists specific suggestions. Staff feel that information should be presented to them more selectively, although all information should be available. To this end they suggest that an index or even library service might be considered. More effective use of briefing meetings to inform staff about products is also needed and this is now under way.

Table 4.6 — **What practical steps should be taken to improve performance for your customers?**

Response	Frequency of response
Facilities	47
Answerphone	
Computer terminals	
Enquiry counter	
Supply of product leaflets	
Viewdata	
More staff	44
More individual attention	
Training	32
Information	23
More information before product release	
More up-to-date information	
Management	21
More authority for cashiers to deal with problems	
More supportive management	
Managers to be available to see customers	
More decisive management	
Staff to feel confident about products	

Table 4.7 — **What practical steps should be taken to improve the information you receive?**

Response	Frequency of response
Organization of information	88
Summaries	
Index	
Library	
Managers to pass on relevant information	
More fact-finders	
Meetings	24
More branch visits	
More regular briefings	
Key-time staff to attend meetings	
Brief staff before customers	
More relevant in-branch product training	

The Staff Meetings

Once the questionnaires were completed, two meetings were held with representative groups of staff to provide the opportunity to discuss the results more fully. The discussions at these meetings powerfully reinforced the picture emerging from the questionnaires. Further clarification was obtained on a number of points.

Training

The staff view is that the external training is good, but they are not always able to put it into practice. In-branch training is poor, partly because of staffing levels. 'It has become more acceptable to make mistakes' was a point widely shared. Pressure on staff had led to increased overtime yet better training might enable junior staff to perform more effectively. More senior staff felt that job knowledge was often poor. Staff also felt that the external training concentrated too much on what to do without advising on how to do it.

Impact of changes

There was a clear perception that staff views were not considered, that information was late and that circulars were often condescending in tone. Viewdata (a data handling software package) was one example of a system which 'arrived' with no preparation or training. Given existing workloads the staff opinion was that many of them might not sell a newly introduced account because of the additional paperwork that would create. Everyone was under pressure. One staff member felt that absenteeism had increased and that this was due to increased pressure.

The change to a sales culture was accepted, but staff questioned whether everyone was able to sell. Nevertheless, they recognized the problem of performance-related pay where job specialization arose. Attitudes here were somewhat cynical. The 'goal-posts' had moved on this scheme. More immediately there was general concern that not all branch managers treated staff in the same way.

An example was given of a staff member who regularly deputized but did not receive deputizing pay because the period involved was always four days rather than the qualifying five days. Other branch managers treated their staff differently.

Work organization

There was a strong recognition that staff skills and experience were not being utilized sufficiently. In particular the senior clerks could do more, have more customer contact and be more involved in team-leading. Branch managers should delegate more. At least one was widely known to open the post and prepare duty lists and dormancy lists. In such a case the branch manager is less accessible to customers and customer service is poor. All staff felt the procedures could be simplified. Many felt that senior clerks should meet to discuss problems, perhaps all visiting the 'best-organized branch in the group' as a means of getting improvements throughout the group.

Management style

Management style was recognized as more human and less distant from people than in the past. People management was judged to have improved and this was helping morale. However, staff felt that managers under-estimated them, did not provide clear or decisive leadership and did not listen. 'Who can you talk to?', 'What will it lead to?' were frequent questions.

Conclusions

The picture that has been portrayed is of a group in which managers and staff are undergoing very significant changes with many more expected. Staff are concerned that these changes are neither well planned nor effectively managed. More fundamentally the attitude changes so important to creating a new sales and performance culture have not yet emerged, at least not consistently. This, however, is to be expected and to ignore that, or to criticize those who have not yet come to terms with the new situation would be to reinforce the constraints which make those attitude changes difficult and time-consuming.

Dramatic changes can be confusing and uncomfortable. Four basic requirements must be met to help people adjust to change:

1. **Empathy** They want people to listen to them, without judging them. The flow of communication must be both ways.

2. **Information** They need to understand why the changes are needed, how they will work, what the impact on themselves will be, i.e. 'What am I trying to deal with?'

3. **Credibility** They need to believe in the changes. They need to be convinced that they will work, will achieve objectives that make sense to them, will resolve problems they see as real. The group plan needs to be communicated effectively.

4. **Ideas for action** They need suggestions for actions, options, plans. They want to put ideas into action, to try them out, to learn from experience. Many of the managers and staff are clear about what is required of them, but not how to achieve a new approach.

Here the evidence collected suggests that there is too much pressure and too much downward communication for many managers and staff to feel that they are listened to or to understand the changes in preparation – too much information, sometimes contradictory and often too late. This means that many do not believe in the changes. Moreover, if anything, the staff see some of the changes as at best irrelevant to the problems they perceive. Overall, whilst many people have ideas for improvement, there is a sense that so much is changing that perhaps it is better to leave things as they are at our level – to not sell a new account!

Recommendations

Using the guidelines set out in the Organizational Diagnosis and the company's implementation sections of the last chapter of this workbook, what recommendation would you make? You should try to identify:

1. A list of specific recommended actions to deal with problems identified by the analysis of suggestions made by managers and staff.

2. Some more general recommendations designed to help the managers cope more effectively with the dramatic changes that are now being experienced at Money Matters plc.

Over the page the recommendations actually implemented are listed. Before turning the page you may find it an interesting exercise to list your own now.

Recommendations

a

b

c

d

e

Specific recommendations

- Review jobs and work organization at branch and departmental level. Ensure that delegation to staff is actively carried out.
- Encourage branch managers to further develop in-branch training on systems and procedures.
- Encourage branch managers to further develop new product briefing meetings with staff.
- Review the role of senior clerks and branch managers regarding in-branch training, staff management, lending and customer contact.
- Examine the use of job rotation of branch managers, partly to encourage delegation, partly as a means of transferring ideas between branches.
- Increase contact between staff. Examine the use of regular meetings of senior clerks to review branch problems – a senior clerk's review group – and to identify areas for improvement.
- Encourage managers to provide positive feedback to staff.
- Group management and branch management to communicate the group plan throughout the organization.
- Clarify and agree a common branch/departmental performance assessment framework based upon the existing systems.

- Ensure greater coordination at group level of meetings, training and requests for returns. Place the onus of responsibility for justifying returns to the staff concerned on the manager asking for them.
- Review the role of quality control.
- Review the presentation of information to managers and staff including the use of indexing and other means of selective provision.
- Review the approach to meetings, reduce the length of presentations and include focused workshop activity where managers can work on group problems and issues.
- Stress counselling should be available to help managers and others cope with the pressure of change. One or more managers should be trained in the essentials of stress counselling with a clear brief to provide help and/ or to refer people on to a more professional source of help should that be needed.

Change Architecture

In this chapter we propose to explore the underlying 'building blocks' of successful change. What are the characteristics of a successful change programme? Is there more to say than the helpful advice one gets in much of the literature? Generally managers are exhorted to 'create a clear vision', to 'engage people in the process', to 'communicate, communicate, communicate', to 'involve people' and so on. All of this is fair enough. But is it enough? In reality organization change and learning are cyclical processes, ideally connected such that a 'virtuous circle' of learning and change can be created. Linear models implying an orderly progression from vision to implementation do not convincingly map out the stops and starts of real life change. Not that by saying this we suggest that progress cannot be achieved. As we said earlier, we reject the overly pessimistic stance of much of the organization change literature, i.e. the 70 per cent of changes fail view. Clearly we also view the change process as comprising a number of processes from 'getting started' to the key process of inclusion of key stakeholders. Is there a body of ideas about the practice of building change programmes which would help us handle change were it to be codified as a change architecture?

Case Study

Technology Associates

If you are the CEO of a global business facing a radical change within tough constraints of competitiveness, revenue instability, dramatic technological change, a rapidly falling share price, investor pressure, legislative issues and so on, what do you do? How do you put together a major change programme if, say, you are ABB employing tens of thousands of people in hundreds of units, businesses etc. across the globe?

Consider the case of Technology Associates. A fictional information management consulting business, wholly owned by a group committed to the manufacture of PCs, other peripherals and software. In recent years the group has dramatically increased the output of its factories and its software development capacity by going to a 24/7 regime (24 hours a day, 7 days a week). Despite the growth of the industry in recent years, this creates substantial pressures on the sales side. Technology Associates, while notionally pursuing a vision of 'customer service' is in fact under pressure to sell solutions to maximize group sales of hardware and software.

This does not mean that its consultants wholly ignore customer needs but nevertheless their bonuses are linked to the sales of group products. Competitors outsource and are therefore less committed to particular configurations. Thus Technology Associates' position has deteriorated.

The board review the situation at a strategy conference: two days away from the day-to-day pressures. It decides upon the need over a period of two years to shift the 'business model' toward the idea of 'outcome based consulting'. A simple enough idea, the change involves focusing the objectives of any consulting engagement more directly on the outcomes defined by the client. The board recognizes that at its core the change involves switching the focus of the engagement away from the pursuit of selling IT configurations. This requires that less attention be focused upon selling particular combinations of hardware and software and more toward jointly defining 'solutions', working with the client on defining and understanding their needs. Ironically in any event this also means changing the focus of the engagement from enhancing low value added sales because competitive pressure has led to the commoditization of hardware and software. Instead the focus was to be on higher value-added outputs – solutions, facilities management, development work, training and so on.

But this change represents first and foremost an intellectual challenge of huge proportions. How to achieve this shift while at the same time continuing to make a valued contribution to those group sales targets is the issue. It is all very well identifying the 'paradigm shift' which is needed, but it is another thing entirely to make that change without destabilizing the parent group.

Moreover to achieve the change, a 'mind set' shift is needed by the consultants themselves. They need new ways of working, new tools and techniques and they must embark on a new world of relationship building and client management.

So how did Technology Associates go about this challenge? Well there are various tasks to undertake as follows:

1. Develop a competence model defining the skills, capabilities and characteristics needed of consultants in order to deploy the new model.
2. Develop a consulting skills workshop as a training and development intervention.
3. Ensure the commitment of managers and consultants to the new business model.
4. Look at existing systems of performance management, people development, coaching, appraisal and rewards to ensure alignment to the new approach.

So let us look at the approach adopted. The Board Strategy Forum was followed by a conference of the board and the regional management teams. With inputs from group, key customers and others, the focus of the conference was on understanding the new vision and working up both a new business model – in outline at least – and an implementation task.

Regional management teams were asked to work on the various systems which would need to be re-aligned and make proposals to a project team. The project team was led by a main board member and reported directly to the board. Each regional management team was represented by the team member deputed to drive forward its own alignment work – see above. A senior HR manager from group was appointed project director on a two-year secondment. The team had a number of consultants involved and through them involved other consultants via a focus group process. There was also outside membership in the project team.

The first task of the project team was to define the competence model. It did so via an open process seeking inputs from consultants in the field and looking at other experience outside the business. Its initial formulations were then tested via panels, both internal and external people, focus groups and regional conferences. As the project team was undertaking this work, the regional team alignment projects acted both as inputs to the process, via the project team process and representation of the regional team member, and took value from the work on the development of the competence model.

The competence model developed, the project team now turned to development of the consulting skills workshop. Several very important decisions were made before any attention was devoted to content. First it was decided that the regional teams would find, from among themselves, the members for the pilot. Also it was agreed that those participants would become the tutors on the consulting skills workshop once it rolled out, accepting that workloads meant that other consultants would also become involved as tutors downstream.

Second a database was designed to support the workshop and activity following the workshop. Participants were committed to making three-month reviews of progress with the new model. In addition a process of best practice exchanges was created using the database and focused activity at regional level incorporated in the existing performance management process.

In outline then let us look at some features of this change architecture:

- Direction from the top is clear enough. The board went into strategy forum mode to work up a new vision and then worked that up into a new business model and implementation plan.
- The project team is clearly accountable to the main board. Its chair is a member of that main board. It utilizes members of the regional teams. The regional teams work on alignment projects which in turn are linked into the work of the project team.
- Regional team members both pilot the consulting skills workshop and become tutors on the roll-out. Thus the company defines its new approach, develops it and works on the changes directly. Outsiders play a role but that of providing benchmarking, advice and questioning – they are not central to the achievement of change.
- A well established process of follow-up is put in place. In particular the database is used to leverage best practice and to target follow-up. It is vital to the achievement of this change that Technology Associates achieve consistency of account management practice. Many of its customers operate globally and may well be dealing with more than one region. In any event inconsistency of account management practice will lead to confusion, inconsistency and poor quality/higher cost in delivery. It seeks to pursue this consistency through the follow-up process.

The project team is also very aware that the initial business model and the consulting skills workshop will be imperfect. Both need revising in the light of experience. The follow-up process provides for the sharing of best practice as a means of doing so. Admittedly not easy to pull off, nevertheless the chances of this follow-up process working effectively is enhanced by designing it as a transparent process and by having the project team responsible for overseeing the process.

More formally then, how would we define the change architecture? Let us look at the following:

- Governance is in place: we are clear how the main board is overseeing the process, and we are clear about the mechanisms through which change is to be implemented.

- Accountability is defined: the project team is accountable to the main board. The regional teams are tasked to work up alignment proposals in support of the project team and therefore, regional teams are engaged but so are other consultants via the process used to develop the competence model.
- Regional team members are engaged in the delivery of the consulting skills workshop.
- The follow-up process seeks to ensure consistency in the application of account management practice and to provide for the leveraging of best practice.
- By using regional team members and other consultants as tutors, the consulting skills workshop process was scaleable – in fact in year one the number of consulting skills workshops rolled out was doubled because of demand from consultants.
- Overall there is a high degree of connectivity between those driving the change, those managing the change processes and those directly affected.
- There is also a considerable degree of transparency of process.
- Whilst it is not completely clear from the above, some attention has been given to the management of expectations throughout the process. In particular the various stages in which internal stakeholders, group (via the project director) and external advisors have been involved, alongside the follow-up process, benchmarking and best practice exchange, all provide for reality checking in terms of the appropriate balance between the external imperatives which must be faced and a realistic view of how quickly change can be achieved within the business.

Note that this external versus internal contrast is far from a straightforward one. While competitive pressure on Technology Associates argues for rapid change, this must be balanced by the view that too rapid a change risks destabilizing the group. Yet, as we have already seen not least in the context of GE, overmuch concern about that can lead to both group and Technology Associates going down. Interestingly enough, the pace of change was ultimately determined by demand from consultants. The original plans were doubled in Year 1 and the roll-out from Europe to the rest of the world was dramatically accelerated. Would this have happened without the transparency of process, level of engagement, connectivity and so on?

Change Architecture Blocks

So far so good! But what can get in the way? Well we have already seen two problems or blocks: our corporate culture can create blocks to a successful change architecture. Simplifying somewhat, the crucial question is not which is the most appropriate corporate culture but rather is it a positive or negative culture? The key issue is that of problem orientation: this is the first block. A positive culture is one within which problems are recognized, discussed and worked on in an open and constructive way. Where problems are not ignored because people might lose 'face' or are felt to be otherwise sensitive to the issue. Where underperformance is not confronted and worked on. Where problem-solving is a 'search for the guilty' rather than for a solution!

The second block relates to inadequate measurement linked to a lack of transparency in performance management. Organizations often rely on inadequate and poorly balanced performance measurement frameworks. In particular this is true in the context of radical change. Almost certainly existing measurement focuses upon finance and activity and on past performance. Clearly this is particularly problematic in the context of change.

But this point can be extended further. I am reminded of something Dwight D Eisenhower, Commander of the Allied Expeditionary Force, D Day and beyond, famously said, 'Before a battle planning is everything: as soon as battle is joined, plans are worthless.'

If plans are worthless once battle is joined, what do we need? A problem oriented process which seeks to deal with the inevitable gaps between original plan and current performance. This demands the training and follow-up we have referred to above.

These ideas find powerful reinforcement in the work of Manzoni (2000). In a study, 'Managerial Behaviour towards Better Performers (BPs) and Weaker Performers (WPs)', Manzoni reports the following:

1. Toward BPs managers tend to:

   - discuss what and why of tasks/projects
   - be open to ideas from BPs
   - spend more time with them
   - give them more challenging tasks.

2. Toward WPs managers tend to:

   - discuss how

- push their own ideas
- monitor actions and results systematically
- be less patient.

3. Various studies show that bosses have 'in-' and 'out-groups' and that bosses probe failure differently.

But does this surprise you? Does it matter? Manzoni argues that subordinate performance tends to adjust to superior's expectations. Thus the danger is that a vicious circle is created. We expect the weaker performer to underperform. Therefore the boss's behaviour is to get involved, to question, to be impatient and to provide less positive reinforcement. In turn this is perceived by the boss as 'doing the job for the WP!' and by the subordinate as 'he doesn't listen/care'. Overall the subordinate feels undervalued, lacking in confidence and esteem and therefore withdraws, behaves mechanically, avoids contact with the boss and so on.

Manzoni calls this 'the set-up to fail syndrome' and it brings various 'costs' as follows:

- worsening performance of WPs
- loss of time and energy of boss
- weaker team
- negative energy
- BPs get increasingly loaded with additional work.

And the syndrome seems more likely to emerge when:

- there is high pressure for results
- short tenures in post
- performance review systems emphasizing a limited range of objectives
- flatter organizations and larger spans of control.

And we have already seen that many of these conditions are either a consequence of value adding organization structures (see Chapter 2) and/ or a clear consequence of radical change.

Gratton (2000) identifies a similar 'cycle of despair' and indicates that she has observed the converse in place at Hewlett Packard. This 'cycle of hope' is created by providing people affected by change with a voice, choice and what she describes as 'interactional justice'. This latter may be about treating people with respect and creating a perception of fair treatment (but see Carnall, 1982 for the complexity of this concept in practice). Be that as it may, we are clearly operating at the intersection between the 'hard' and 'soft' world of organization. Just as clearly many of the problems in handling change emerge out of inadequate management and infrastructure, and thus it is that we argue for change architecture to deal with these problems amongst others.

Gratton's book (2000) is relevant because she develops an idea of strategy methodology that relates closely to the change architecture thinking presented here. For Gratton creating a 'living strategy' requires six steps:

1. **Step 1: Creating a guiding coalition**
   She identifies five key sets of stakeholders, namely senior managers, HR professionals, young people, line managers, front line staff. Each brings a unique perspective.

2. **Step 2: Visioning the future**
   She limits herself to visioning the people issues in this step. Thus she recounts how at Phillips Lighting the senior executives team presented strategic goals, i.e. grow to 25 per cent market share, No. 1 choice in Europe, No. 2 in rest of the world, No. 1 in customer satisfaction, and so on which became a frame of reference for visioning teams. In turn these visioning teams identified the organizational factors with a high impact on the delivery of that vision – namely a structure capable of delivering new business and a network-driven organization.

3. **Step 3: Identifying gaps**
   Understanding the current position and identifying gaps. She presents a risk matrix, essentially a 2 dimensional model mapping strategic impact against current alignment.

4. **Step 4: Mapping**
   Identify key themes, i.e. customer focus, innovation, globalization and market share, identify change levers, i.e. selection, rewards, training, development, identify desired end-states and model the dynamics.

5. **Step 5: Modelling the dynamics of the vision**
   This final step looks at implementation. She identifies two principles of interest to us.

6. **Step 6: Bridging into action**

   i   Making changes to move HR strategy forward. Leverage with processes and behaviours and values will follow. She argues that values and 'meanings' are outcomes of change, not levers to create change.

   ii Understanding the forces for and against change, in essence the force field idea (see Chapter 7).

Interestingly for this review of change architecture, Gratton argues that the journey forward to create new strategy includes four further guiding principles:

- Continue to build guiding coalitions.
- Build the capacity to change.
- Keep focusing on the themes.
- Build performance measures noting that leading measures are in the field of people development, behaviour and attitudes, living measures are of performance and lagging measures include financial performance.

This is too simplistic. To argue that leading measures are only to be found in measures to do with people is just wrong. If you are looking at an engineering business quite obviously technology capabilities are important as leading measures. Could the success or failure of the Wellcome Trust funded Human Genome Project be judged at the point of committing funding only or even largely on the characteristics of people – many of whom were not yet involved? Could you assess whether or not to fund a Mars project with NASA by looking only at people issues? This is just too narrow. It argues that we replace one extreme with another. Nevertheless there is a sense running through the approach that you do need to have regard to the design of the strategy and, by implication, the strategic change process.

Is there a difference between engagement and involvement? We argue that this is so. For example if I ask someone to send me their views on a particular topic, I seek to gain their engagement with the topic and the issues involved. But I have not sought to involve them in the process of debate, dialogue, decision making and so on. We could only describe this as an example of involvement by defining the latter too widely to be useful. Again if I ask someone to think about the implications for them of a particular change prior to a career counselling discussion, I am seeking to engage their thinking about the change without involving them.

The distinction is important in this sense. When we talk of the need to communicate during a period of change we often argue that communication must be two way. In practice this is often not the reality, because we provide little real opportunity for the feedback process. However, modern practice increasingly provides for feedback, email 'speak-ups', 'town meetings' etc. Thus we suggest that one can think of communication as a process for cascading messages about vision, objectives, plans and progress. Engagement refers to attempts to get either feedback or ideas – we seek to stimulate thinking about the changes. Involvement relates to bringing people into task forces, working groups, focus groups and the like.

Any given set of proposals for change have two important contexts, the change drivers – the forces impacting on the vision, strategy change ideas and so on – and the change architecture itself. The drivers for change include the rate of change in the economy and the business sector environment, current performance and stakeholders' views and the degree of ambition in the proposals. The change architecture is as previously described. The two combined will lead to higher or lower feelings of confidence in the outcome amongst key stakeholders. If confidence is low then there will likely be behaviours that are unhelpful. Conversely where confidence is high, positive behaviour is more likely. But the links are likely to be curvilinear. Too modest or too extreme an approach on the change drivers' side is similarly likely to lead to negatives. For example, if the degree of ambition is seen not to measure up to the challenge in the environment or if the degree of ambition is high but the change architecture is poorly developed.

These ideas are set out in Figure 5.1. Here we suggest that success in change management requires integration of the changes in the organization, effective performance management and effective project management of the change programme. By performance management we refer to the performance management of the organization at large, not just of the change programme. By integration we are saying that the project management of the change programme must be integrated with the performance management of the organization – something only rarely achieved in practice albeit new approaches to performance measurement, i.e. the 'balanced scorecard' make that easier.

For these processes to be in place related to any given change and to be seen to work there are three sets of critical dimensions for us to consider:

1. **The level of ambition and risk:** clearly the more ambitious the changes attempted the less likely we are to succeed? Perhaps not strictly true. It may be that the relationship is curvilinear – a lower likelihood of success for very low levels and very high levels of ambition. Nevertheless this question of ambition/risk must factor into the analysis.

2. **The available 'strategic assets', 'organization infrastructure' and 'knowledge infrastructure':** in effect here we are referring to the existing resources and competencies. If these are strong then the chances of success are higher, all other things being equal.

3. **Finally the change architecture:** these are the dimensions we can work with as part of the change management task.

Figure 5.1   Change architecture

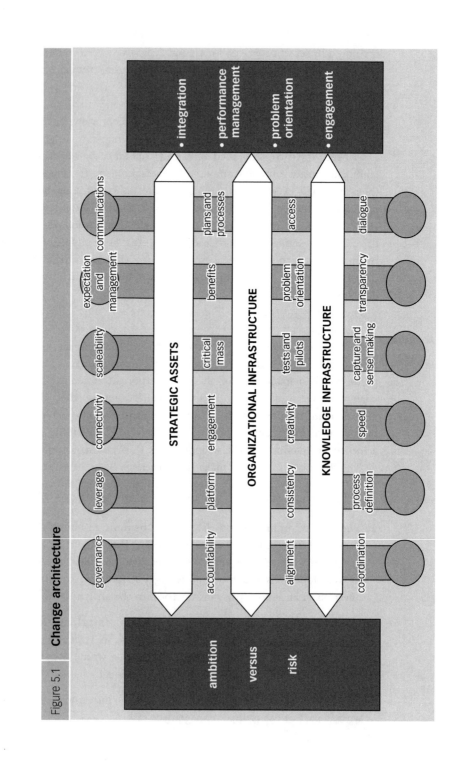

Taking the dimensions of change architecture in turn we can look at the elements for each dimension as set out in the toolkit.

Change Architecture Exercise

Change architecture toolkit

Toolkit

	Not at All				Fully in Place
	1	2	3	4	5
1. Governance					
1.1 Accountability for all parts of the Change process is clear.	▦	▦	▦	▦	▦
1.2 All efforts, tasks, processes required to progress the change are aligned in terms of planned outcomes.	▦	▦	▦	▦	▦
1.3 All efforts of individuals and groups involved are co-ordinated.	▦	▦	▦	▦	▦
2. Leverage					
2.1 'Platforms' of resources, skills and knowledge are available for the deployment of new systems, processes, initiatives etc.	▦	▦	▦	▦	▦
2.2 All elements of the change are being implemented consistently.	▦	▦	▦	▦	▦
2.3 Full value (for the change) is being gained from existing assets and resources.	▦	▦	▦	▦	▦
3. Connectivity					
3.1 Key stakeholders are being engaged appropriately.	▦	▦	▦	▦	▦
3.2 The process of change is being managed creatively, new ideas are welcomed.	▦	▦	▦	▦	▦
3.3 Resources allow the change process to be handled with speed.	▦	▦	▦	▦	▦

	Not at All				Fully in Place
	1	2	3	4	5
4. Scaleability					
4.1 A critical mass of capabilities, competence and support is emerging/ being developed.	▢	▢	▢	▢	▢
4.2 Use is being made of pilots, tests and simulations to test out and learn new ideas and techniques.	▢	▢	▢	▢	▢
4.3 New systems are being codified, process definition is being developed, learning is being captured.	▢	▢	▢	▢	▢
5. Management of expectations					
5.1 Benefits are clear and identified	▢	▢	▢	▢	▢
5.2 The change process is being handled in a 'problem-oriented' way.	▢	▢	▢	▢	▢
5.3 There is transparency in change management.	▢	▢	▢	▢	▢

Some will immediately argue on the basis of where are the people issues and what about communication. The individual and team dynamics of change are important and are dealt with elsewhere in the book. This is not to diminish the importance of those issues related to their impact on people, resistance to change and so on. Rather here we present the notion that those issues are more readily handled if an effective change architecture is in place. Similarly on communication. You might include it as a sixth dimension of the change architecture however, and were we to do so it would look like the following.

	Not at All				Fully in Place
	1	2	3	4	5
6. Communication					
6.1 A communication plan for change is in place dealing with:					
6.1.1 Progress and performance	▢	▢	▢	▢	▢

	Not at All				Fully in Place
	1	**2**	**3**	**4**	**5**
6. Communication (continued)					
6.1.2. Future plans and intentions	▦	▦	▦	▦	▦
6.1.3 Consultation on key issues yet to be resolved.	▦	▦	▦	▦	▦
6.2 The plan provides clear access opportunities for individuals/teams to make their views known and get information/updates.	▦	▦	▦	▦	▦
6.3 Arrangements exist to capture, analyse and make sense of the communication to help better understand the changes going forward.	▦	▦	▦	▦	▦

Enabling Infrastructure

To my mind the first topic to get straight is that of culture. Can corporate cultures be changed? Some say 'yes' but only with major effort and over a long period of time. If you accept that view you may well see culture change as an objective achievable only in the longer term of other changes, with the idea that we need to move toward more adaptive cultures.

Marriott Hotels

Marriott's work ethic focused on a philosophy of 'see and be seen'. To be seen as loyal and committed people felt the need to be seen to work long hours. While perhaps never something people were comfortable with, the new generation of younger managers was increasingly clear that work-life balance is a real issue. In turn the hotel was finding it hard to recruit and retain talented people, not least because of this issue.

As a change issue this is tough. You are dealing with deeply ingrained behaviour, i.e. with a culture change issue. These changes are particularly difficult to handle. Yet not least of the issues facing the hotel is the clear contrast between 'face time', i.e. being seen to be there – a ritualistic process, and being genuinely effective as a business. Can a business run on face time be a business that values its people?

In early 2000 Marriott implemented a test programme called 'Management Flexibility' at three hotels. This was projected as a six-month pilot. Early on there were to be some easy gains via the review of meetings and procedures. Success was to be measured on four criteria: working hours, job-related stress, financial performance (no adverse impact) and sustained service levels. The pilots were initiated by meetings with the senior teams in the pilot hotels. A consulting firm ran a series of focus groups involving 165 managers from the pilot hotels. These focus groups identified procedure changes of various kinds, each of which avoided inefficiencies

Case Study

and/or duplications of effort, thus saving time. In some cases proposals were brought forward relating to the use of tools such as the Internet-email and so on. Regular meetings were reviewed and either discontinued or scaled down.

Perhaps more importantly the senior teams at the pilot hotels began to articulate the new way of working. This was not about working shorter hours as such but rather about not equating working with 'being in the hotel'. The message was about achieving your objectives, meeting your commitments and delivering value to customers – not face time.

Three months into the pilot people were no longer joking about long work hours. Employee surveys showed significant attitude change during the pilot. Also before the pilot, managers had reported spending an average of nearly 12 hours per week on low value work and this fell to less than seven hours. Yet other data showed that customers' perception of service was unchanged and performance had not declined – indeed there were gains (Munch, 2001).

Clearly then it is possible to change long embedded practices, ways of thinking and perceiving. By implication at least this does suggest that there are ways of achieving culture change as a derivative of other changes falling into place.

Some appear to believe that you can operate directly upon corporate culture, but most of what I would see as current best practice focuses upon putting in place behavioural and other changes to pursue longer term culture change. Thus Thornberry (1999) shows us how KPMG sought to 'revitalise its culture through values'. Here culture change was led by one person as part of the ongoing management development programme within KPMG. Ultimately she calls for 'pragatism' and 'practical steps to implementation'.

The approach was in three stages: diagnosis, visioning a new culture and implementation, and a toolkit approach was adopted globally and modified by each country or local practice. Much of the focus was on identifying behaviour, but much of the process was located in a management game called 'The Values Game' and a boxed set of tools including 'Implementation Guide', 'Leadership Alignment', 'Personal and Team Development', 'Communications', 'Process Management' (providing methods for running events, conducting research, measuring progress) and some content papers providing theoretical background. The focus was upon who we are, what we believe in, what we do and what we need to change. Via diagnosis, visioning and discussion the purpose was to so re-orientate behaviour that via positive reinforcement new values and a new corporate culture would emerge.

Whenever you look at culture change programmes, you will see a pattern of this type. The focus is upon the cognitive and behavioural worlds – on how we understand what we do, think, aspire to, how we behave and the consequences of our behaviour. Culture change is derivative of other changes.

Does this mean that we cannot achieve the active management of culture? In one sense 'no', and we shall see how shortly, but first let us look at the definition of culture. In fact there are a multiplicity of definitions dealing with terms such as 'assumptions', 'perceptions', 'patterns of meanings', 'symbols', 'values'. Moreover culture is seen as 'socially constructed' and arising out of, for example, the company context – markets, technology – the structures and functions – centralized versus decentralized structures.

What is agreed about culture is that it is

- difficult to define
- multi-dimensional
- changing
- leads to major misunderstandings when cultures 'collide'
- culture shock can be real
- can either be positive or negative
- takes time to build.

Crucially, what is not clear is: whether we should celebrate cultural diversity as a source of innovation or not.

Many different culture classification systems exist including geographical, economic, historical, linguistic, religio-political, but for our purposes value based, organizational based and socially defined classification systems are most frequently used. For example the following authors have coined the following types of classifications.

Hofstede (1988)	power distance
	masculinity-femininity
	individualism-collective
	uncertainty avoidance
Deal and Kennedy (1982)	macho
	work hard – play hard
	bet-your-company
	process
Schein (1992)	power
(similar to Handy (1976)	role
and Harrison (1970))	achievement
	support

When thinking about the management of people, culture impacts on these processes:

- getting in – recruitment process
- breaking in – encounter stage
- settling in – metamorphosis stage.

Other processes impacted by culture:

- planning
- formal versus informal
- short versus long term
- explicit versus implicit
- career management
- appraisal and compensation
- selection and induction.

These authors mentioned above provide questionnaire based 'measures' of culture, but for our purpose the most interesting approach is that adopted by Goffee and Jones (1998) who present a questionnaire measure of culture but go on to look at whether any of the four cultures they define are positive or negative. This seems an important key to practical work in the change management field. It may take years to change the culture (the derivative change point), but if we can create a positive or problem oriented approach we may be more likely to achieve change whatever the culture. In turn these changes, if reinforced, will ultimately lead to culture change.

Adaptive organization is required because we need to transform the way we do our business, as seen in Table 6.1.

The matrix in Table 6.1 looks at the focus of both top level executives and experienced managers, or middle managers more generally, for both business as usual plus and transformational changes. In both, a problem oriented approach is important, but in transformational change the ambiguity, risk levels and uncertainty require the radical rethinking referred to above which is what will lead to derivative culture change. Rethinking means or leads to learning, thus transformational change requires executives focused on 'leading learning'.

Strategic change is about both leadership and learning. In an increasingly volatile environment leadership is an increasingly challenging process or attribute or bundle of ideas, attributes and behaviours. Of course this reflects both our current preoccupation with leadership and the varying views about what leadership means in practice. But while we expect leaders to play the pivotal role in articulating strategic vision for the organization

Table 6.1	**Toward transformational change?**	
	Business as Usual Plus	Adaptive Organization/Transformational Change
	Top Level	Leading in Ambiguity
	Performance driven and continuous improvement	Transformational leadership
		Significant risk-taking
	Competitive Pressures	Creating case for change
	Leading managers and Professionals	Create environment to enable change
	Managing large organizations and functions	Shift towards personal powerbase
	Create strategy	
	Experienced Manager	Implementing transformational change
	Performance driven, clear targets	Speed of change
	Competitive environment	Ambiguity
	Manage within limits	Working with limited knowledge
	Manage projects	Project management
	Manage within networks	Communicating someone else's message
		Increased complexity

and in achieving that vision, our approach also seeks to create space and scope for the engagement and/or involvement of others, principally ourselves! Also given the volatility of today's world, we recognize that learning is vital to all of this if we are to get it right.

Meyerson (2001) talks about people who eschew confrontational approaches for incremental attempts to challenge the status quo from within. These she calls 'tempered radicals' because they seek significant changes in moderate ways. She shows that such people can use a range of approaches to change their organizations, but the crucial argument is that leadership from within the organization working within codes of behaviour and structure can still challenge all of that in a constructive fashion and achieve significant changes.

Edmonson, Bohmer and Pisaro (2001) look at how 'learning leaders' can accelerate teams adapting to new ways of working. A learning leader is accessible, asks for input and demonstrates fallibility, i.e. is willing to own up to mistakes. In effect they explicitly manage for learning. The 'tempered radical' behaves in ways which are consistent with this model. Thus they are people who ask radical questions in an undramatic way. They act convincingly rather than destructively.

Often, therefore, multi-disciplinary activities will form part of the process we create to develop new visions and change. These activities may variously include board away days, strategy forums, top level conferences and change workshops. But the purpose is to create a sharing of ideas, perspectives and dialogue. Sharing of ideas and perspectives because we recognize that internal and external stakeholders possess relevant ideas, views and experiences which will help both in the formation of change proposals and in the positioning of those proposals in the debate about the future of the business – always part of any significant change process.

Change Management Workshops – Some Evidence

Multi-disciplinary workshops are a commonly used technique within change programmes. Often a company going through a major change will organize many such workshops. Sometimes they will be organized on behalf of the company either by a consulting firm or by a business school. Often they will be run by the company through its own resources. Yet if you read the change management literature it is clear that such workshops are rarely studied. Very little is revealed in quite major studies about the design, process or operation of these workshops, still less is there any evaluation presented.

Yet well-known authors clearly believe such workshops to be of real importance. For example Beckhard and Pritchard (1992) describe a 'vision-driven change effort' at Statoil in Norway. A key stage of the process developed as follows:

> The top managers have set up a series of meetings to develop and jointly review the corporate values and principles for managing and acting. The meetings include the top management team, and other senior managers, as participants. The top leaders believe that, as with the vision, it is crucial for these values and principles to be 'owned' by the entire senior management. They hope the outcome of these meetings will be a commitment by the organization's leaders to use these principles and values as the guide to their behaviour.

So one obvious purpose of change workshops is to gain commitment, 'buy-in' and a sense of ownership. Later on these authors discuss the role of 'educational intervention' as part of managing organizational change, arguing that they can both aid understanding of the change problem and build commitment.

Vince (1996) provides an evaluation of a research/training process undertaken to develop action plans to support good practice in equal opportunity policy and practice in a public sector employment agency. Workshops played an important part of the process and evidently participants felt that they had learned about equal opportunities from the process. They were just as clear that the workshops ought to have been led by senior executives rather than solely by trainers. Whilst the data is not clear, nevertheless it appears that the latter point reflects a concern about the post workshop period – will there be commitment from the top?

At another level of concern, Ellinor and Gerard (1998) show how the use of dialogue can help people talk through issues in ways conducive to change and transformation. At its core they define two forms of dialogue:

1. Convergent conversation, which narrows discussion down toward the one best perspective, opinion and answer, and

2. Divergent conversation, which expands discussion by allowing for a multiplicity of perspectives.

The crux of this is to engage in each at the appropriate time, the latter early on in the change workshop process. In turn these authors suggest the following processes as important:

1. Listening – focus on shared meanings

   - release outcomes
   - respect differences.

2. Suspend judgement – balance inquiry and advocacy

   - speak when moved
   - suspend roles and status
   - speak to the group.

3. Inquiry and reflection – listen without resistance

   - share responsibility
   - go live.

Herein is the beginning of an evaluative framework with which to think about the process within a series of change management workshops. However to do so directly would require observational methodologies which are both expensive and likely also to impact on the workshop process, so we are not likely to get direct evidence at this level of detail.

Cope (1996) presents a useful study of what he calls 'staged events' used to mobilize change. He reports an evaluation study of one programme of staged events undertaken within a global telecommunications business. Both participants and the workshop 'owner' were interviewed. The interviews were transcribed and the resulting 158 items emerging from a content analysis were combined into 14 categories, which he uses to describe the role of the staged event. Out of this came a model in which the changes to be mobilized are articulated through the staged event via pre-event, event and post-event processes.

Emery and Purser (1996), Bunker and Alban (1996) and Jacobs (1994) describe the use of conference and small group methods within change processes along similar lines, like looking at issues such as the critical mass of involvement, participative processes as a means of achieving inclusion and a sense of community. Of particular relevance to us is the concept of 'soak time'. Bunker and Alban (1996) for example are clear that if dramatically new ideas are presented then people need time to reflect on them, in this context arguing the need for at least two nights 'sleeping over the issues' as part of the process. One can see that it will take people time to reframe their own ideas in the context of new ideas and that this will not happen immediately and must be designed into the process.

Jacobs (1994) describes a sequence of three processes that go on in change workshops:

1. building a common data base on the issues

2. discovering the future through diverse perspectives

3. creating commitments and action plans.

Clearly therefore the process requires a substantial period of dialogue before attempts are made to close the process down even though participants may seek closure more quickly.

Similarly Norlton (1998) reports on change workshops she has managed in New Zealand. Here workshop evaluations indicated that early on participants point to closure, future plans, application, achieving change, while at the same time celebrating the sharing of ideas, their own inclusion, the value of the process and so on. All of this points to the notion that change workshops dealing with fundamental changes need to be at least three days long, should be facilitated to maintain dialogue for at least two of those days but also need to be focused upon the post-workshop application period. Ironically, the process needs to focus on maintaining the dialogue while the design of the workshop needs to pivot on what will happen next and how.

Learning Strategies for Managing Complex Change

Neumann, Holti and Standing (1995) describe the Tavistock Institute of Management methodology for planning and sequencing comprehensive change. Whilst they apply it only to projects concerned in developing teamworking, in a manufacturing context it is relevant to this discussion because it is offered as a means of coping with continual change in everything in the workplace. They claim the methodology is particularly relevant in circumstances such as uncertainty about the environment, the 'guiding values' of the organization or about connections and impacts with other aspects of the business.

Their methodology comprises five steps, through which large group and intergroup intervention strategies are used. The steps are:

1. Map issues and identify broad areas for initiative, identifying importance and urgency.

2. Identify a set of interconnected and compatible initiatives for more detailed planning and sequencing.

3. Clarify initial actions, the decisions needed, any uncertainties which hinder choice and arranging for further work.

4. Agree a 'progress package' of actions and other work across the whole organization.

5. Establish cross-departmental working groups to progress Step 4 and agree the next large group review.

The vital points about this methodology are two-fold. First, there is explicit reference to the idea of connections or connectivity (see our discussion of change architecture in Chapter 4). Second the process is about dialogue and openness and there is a concern to sequence activity.

Dialogue and openness within a framework of the type these authors propose is about leading and learning. No-one is assumed to know all the answers. We make explicit the notion of dilemmas. There may be no ultimate or perfect solution, only ways of making progress. As they argue: 'The continuing, longer-term process engages the organization in developing as a learning organization, in which cultural resistance to achieving the purposes can be worked through'.

All of the above suggests that change makes very specific demands on 'leaders'. Higgs and Rowland (2000) discuss how to 'build change leadership capability' via the definition of change competencies. They report an initial research study undertaken in a major multi-national company wherein the 'client' organization had posed the researchers questions related to the role of the 'leader in change' and the involvement of others in leading the change process. They identify eight change management competencies:

1. change initiation

2. change impact

3. change facilitation

4. change leadership

5. change learning

6. change execution

7. change presence

8. change technology.

They report the use of this model in change management workshops and discuss the relatively positive response in the company to this work. In a subsequent publication (Higgs and Rowland, 2001) they report early results from this research from which they present evidence that there were both identifiable impact on change competence as assessed via peer and manager ratings and positive business impact from the change programmes of which this competence development work was a part. Note however that the sample size was small, only 11 managers were involved, and also that they present no direct evidence of a link between enhanced change competence and the business impact of change. Thus the research is at best suggestive of a link, however it does represent a first attempt to look at this problem in research terms.

Lufthansa

In the eight years up to 1999 Lufthansa proceeded from the verge of bankruptcy to record results and becoming a founder member of the Star Alliance, a global network of airline companies and others. Following the initial restructuring to avoid financial collapse, the executive board and the supervisory board decided upon a process of strategic renewal, fundamental to which was a process of 'mental change'.

In early 1992 Lufthansa found itself with only 14 days of operating cash available with little prospect of support from the banking system. Having engineered a short-term solution, it embarked upon a four week change management programme for Lufthansa executives out of which emerged a group committed to radical change and who became known as 'Samurai of Change'. In mid-1992, 20 senior managers participated in a meeting initially known as 'Mental Change', but which became known as the 'Crisis Management Meeting'. This meeting created 'Program 93' – 131 projects or actions leading to 8000 job cuts, fleet downsizing, revenue enhancement efforts and so on.

The executive board appointed task forces to implement these projects, mostly headed by members of the 'Samurai of Change'. To communicate this, Lufthansa adopted General Electric's 'town meetings'. By mid-1999 the CEO had participated in over 200 such meetings.

Progress of the 131 projects was monitored under the direction of the corporate financial controller using explicit measures of revenue growth and cost reduction. By 1995 the results of this work were apparent throughout the group, setting the scene for more fundamental restructuring from a functional structure to a federal structure comprising decentralized business units. Subsequently 'Programme 15' was implemented from 1996, focusing upon strategic cost management aimed at cutting costs by 20 per cent in five years. The 'Program 15' Task Force emphasized the vital need for transparency and measurement as a means of progress managing major change. Line managers are responsible for the implementation of 'Program 15' cost reductions, all of which are integrated within their objectives and form part of their performance evaluation.

The underlying principles of this change effort were as follows:

- reduce communication costs and simplify decision making
- support corporate-wide task force working
- support the Lufthansa Service Initiative via service-focused workshops.

Perhaps more important is the change architecture implemented around the various change projects. Performance management was used explicitly to drive change forward. Feedback systems – customer surveys, employee commitment surveys, 360° feedback tools and customer and employee short surveys, 'pulsetakers' – were used to get feedback around the group. Programmes such as 'Explorer 21' and 'Climb 99' initiatives run within the Lufthansa Business School became an explicit part of the culture change process. Involving 210 and 160 managers/young professionals respectively, these programmes represent both investment in learning and development and culture change. The vital word is integration or leverage. Such activities became seen as 'transformation platforms' for change providing the prospect of achieving a critical mass of change. Starting from self-assessment using customized leadership tools, the programmes are a means of learning by 'contributing to the future of the business'. By the year 2000 many thousands of Lufthansa employees had been involved in one or more activities related to strategic changes (Bruch and Sattelberger, 2001).

Pulling the thinking together, the Lufthansa case study shows how a radical approach based upon rethinking the business model followed by the use of a well organized change architecture can lead to culture change. More importantly it shows that change management needs to deal with more than the 'behavioural world'. While the behaviours of leaders in a change situation make a difference, this needs to be balanced by the cognitive aspects. Is the change relevant? Is it understood? Is it credible? Unless mind sets are changed all the behaviour change in the world will not create success, thus the substantial effort within the change architecture in use to link the learning and service development initiatives to the work of the 'Program 15' Task Force. Learning around the new business model for the modern Lufthansa can be most effectively developed through practical work within, say, 'Explorer 21'. Thus a development programme such as Explorer 21 is integrated with the changes under way by being leveraged as part of the activity supporting Program 15.

7

Building Effective Change Initiatives

The final chapter focuses upon three sets of change management tools:

1. Implementation exercise – designed to help you think through implementation in some detail.

2. Change management skills – focuses upon your own personal change management/leadership development needs.

3. Change risk – looks at the likelihood of successful and sustainable implementation of change.

Implementation Exercise

This exercise comprises two checklists. The checklists are designed to help you think about aspects of the organization that might help or hinder the implementation of change. Please complete the two checklists by focusing on a significant organizational change in which you have been or are now involved. Fill in details of the change on the next page before turning to the checklists.

Objectives:

Scope and type of change (e.g. reorganization, new product, new technology):

Who is affected and how:

Timetable for implementation:

Checklist 1: Readiness for change

Please tick the appropriate statement				
1. In the past new policies or systems introduced by management have been:	Seen as meeting employees' needs ▨	Not well understood ▨	Greeted with some resistance ▨	Vigorously resisted ▨
2. Employees may be best described as:	Innovative ▨	Independent ▨	Apathetic ▨	Conservative or resistant to change ▨
3. The most recent and widely known change in the organization is viewed as:	A success ▨	Moderately successful ▨	Had no obvious impact ▨	Not successful ▨
4. Expectations of what change will lead to are:	Consistent throughout the organization ▨	Consistent amongst senior management but not otherwise ▨	Not at all consistent ▨	Unclear ▨
5. What can people directly affected by the changes tell you about the organization's business or strategic plan?	A full description ▨	A description of where it affects their own department or activity ▨	A general idea ▨	Nothing ▨
6. Outcomes of the change have been:	Specified in detail ▨	Outlined in general terms ▨	Poorly defined ▨	Not defined ▨
7. Present work procedures to be affected by the change are seen as needing:	Major change ▨	Significant alteration ▨	Minor ▨	No change ▨

8. The problems to be dealt with by the change were first raised by:	The people directly involved	First-line management and supervision	Senior management	Outside consultants
9. The proposed change is viewed by end users as:	Crucial to the organization's future	Generally beneficial to the organization	Beneficial only to part of the organization	Largely a matter of procedure
10. Top management support for the proposed change is:	Enthusiastic	Limited	Minimal	Unclear
11. Top management has:	Committed significant resources to the change	Expects the change to be implemented from existing resources	Has withheld resources	Has not planned the resources needed
12. The management performance appraisal and review process is:	An important part of management development	A helpful problem solving process	Routine	An obstacle to improvement
13. The proposed change deals with issues of relevance to the business plan:	Directly	Partly	Only indirectly	Not at all
14. The proposed change:	Makes jobs more rewarding financially and otherwise	Makes jobs easier and more satisfying	Replaces old tasks and skills with new ones	Makes jobs harder
15. The proposed change is technically:	Similar to others already under way	Similar to others undertaken in the recent past	Novel	Unclear technically

Checklist 2: Managing change

Please tick the appropriate statement			
1. The implementation plan provides:	Clear targets ▪	Acceptable targets ▪	Broad objectives ▪	No targets ▪
2. The likelihood of project deadlines being met is:	High ▪	Moderate ▪	Low ▪	Non-existent ▪
3. Day-to-day control of implementation is being managed by:	One specific person ▪	Several people ▪	No one specific individual ▪	Not sure ▪
4. Implementation begins in:	One small work area or department ▪	A number of units ▪	A major department or division ▪	Throughout the organization ▪
5. The plan is being introduced:	Almost 'overnight' ▪	Rapidly ▪	Gradually ▪	Very slowly ▪
6. Those involved initially were selected:	Because they were flexible and supportive ▪	Because they were very committed to the organization ▪	Because they most needed the change ▪	No reason ▪
7. Training is being carried forward with:	Outside training only ▪	Specially designed sessions in-house plus outside training ▪	Technical or user manuals ▪	Not at all ▪
8. Training is designed to:	Solve problems with the new system ▪	Involve the user's experience ▪	Designed for a wide range of audience ▪	Takes no account of users ▪

9. Training involves:	Only key end users or those affected	Involves everyone affected	Does not involve end users	No training provided
10. Implementation of the change will:	Allow people full control of the tasks they perform	Help people better control the tasks they do	Mean that tasks are controlled by the 'system' or the technology	Control the people performing the tasks
11. Managers discuss changes with users and others:	To develop the plans for change	To get ideas and feedback on implementation	To keep them informed	To control progress
12. Implementation has:	Built-in incentives and rewards	Provision for some recognition of success	No specific incentives	Problems for the people using the system
13. Benefits will occur:	Immediately	Quickly	Within a year of implementation	Over a year following implementation
14. Direct benefits will be:	Clearly apparent to users	Apparent only to managers	Apparent only to top managers	Only indirect benefits
15. Effects will be:	Measurable in quantitative terms	Measurable only as 'ratings'	Largely anecdotal	Not clear
16. During change people need to put in:	Very considerable effort, skill and extra work	Considerable effort, skill and extra work	Some extra effort, skill and work	No extra effort, skill or work
17. Management provides people with:	Excellent support	Good support	Limited support	No support

Toolkit

18. People experience:	High levels of pressure or stress during change	Considerable pressure or stress during change	Some pressure or stress during change	No stress during change
	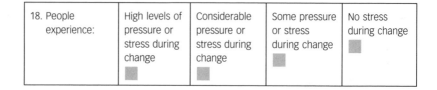			

The two checklists deal with a range of implementation problems. Set out below is a summary of the techniques and principles that can be applied to alleviate these implementation problems. Each box lists questions related to a set of three points in one of the two checklists. If you tend to select the third or fourth option for completing a statement in any group of three points, then it would be worth reviewing the relevant techniques for your own organization.

Methods for Implementing Change

Checklist 1: readiness for change

To deal with resistance to change (points 1–3)

- Has there been unsuccessful past experience of change?
- Do we have a risk-averse culture?
- Are there communication problems?

Keep everyone informed by making information available and explaining plans clearly, allowing access to management for questions and clarification. Ensure that change is sold realistically by making a practical case for change; explain change in terms which the employee will see as relevant and acceptable; show how change fits business needs and plans and spend time and effort on presentations.

Prepare carefully by making a full organizational diagnosis; spend time with people and groups, building trust, understanding and support.

Involve people by getting feedback on proposals; get people to fill out the checklists and discuss the data from these checklists.

Start small and build success by piloting a receptive group of employees in departments with a successful track record and implement changes in clear phases.

Plan for success by starting with changes that can give a quick and positive pay-off; publicize early success and provide positive feedback to those involved in success.

To clarify the effects of change (points 4–6)

- What are people's expectations of change?
- What are the objectives of change?

Clarify the benefits of changes by emphasizing the benefits to those involved and to the company. Emphasize where the new systems utilize existing knowledge and skills. Minimize surprises by specifying all assumptions about the change; focus on the outcomes and identify potential problems.

Communicate plans by being specific in terms familiar to the different groups of employees; communicate periodically and through various media; ask for feedback; do not suppress negative views but listen to them carefully and deal with them openly.

To identify ownership of change (points 7–9)

- Are procedures, systems, departments, products and services seen as a problem?
- Who planned the changes – top management or a staff department?

Plan for visible outcomes from change. Clarify employees' views by exploring their concerns about the changes and examining impact on the day-to-day routines. Specify who wants change and why; explain longer term advantages; identify common benefits and present the potential of change.

To ensure top management support (points 10–12)

- Will top management support the changes openly?
- Will top management provide the necessary resources?
- Is the management performance appraisal process an obstacle to change?

Build a power base by becoming the expert in the problems involved; understand top management concerns; develop information and formal support; develop a strong and polished presentation in top management language.

Develop clear objectives and plans by establishing a clear timetable; set up review processes to be supportive, involving top management and middle management and focus meetings on specific outcomes and specific problems.

To create acceptance of changes (points 13–15)

- Do the planned changes fit other business plans?
- Is there a clear sense of direction?

- Do the proposed changes place greater demands on people?
- Does the change involve new technology or expertise?

Identify relevance of change to plans by reviewing plans and specifying how change fits; incorporate changes into ongoing developments and if possible, frame changes in terms of the organization's style.

Implement changes using flexible or adaptable people, who are familiar with some or all of the change in a part of the business where there are strong supporters for change and recognize why people support change (career, rewards, company politics).

Do not oversell change. Be clear about conflicts with present practices and encourage discussion of these conflicts.

To build an effective team to implement change (points 16–18)

- Will team members be inflexible in dealing with change?
- Will managers need to work hard to ensure commitment to changes?

Ensure that teams have clear and agreed goals. Involve all members of the team in ways they each see as relevant that use their own skills/expertise. Be prepared to face and deal with conflict. Encourage constructive feedback.

Checklist 2: managing change

To clarify plans for change (points 1–3)

- Do we have clear plans, deadlines and milestones?
- Is there clear accountability?
- Do we have a realistic timetable?

Assign one person to be accountable overall for change and ensure clear accountability at all levels.

Define goals carefully by checking feasibility with people involved, experts and other companies and use measurable goals where possible but always looking at broader goals and outcomes.

Define specific goals by defining small, clear steps, identifying and publicizing critical milestones and assign firm deadlines.

Translate plans into action by publishing plans; build in rewards for performance and give regular feedback.

To build new systems and practices into the organization (points 4–6)

- How wide is the scope/scale of change?
- Are people supportive, informed, prepared?

Plan the rate of change carefully by piloting to learn from experience; implement for success, small steps and specific milestones and allow *more* time.

Enlist firm support and ensure that new procedures, products and services are well understood.

To provide training and support (points 7–9)

- Are we providing specific, relevant training?
- Is the training flexible and geared to people's needs?
- Is the training supported in the work place?
- Are we targeting the right people for training?

Clarify objectives of training; use existing skills and knowledge; depend on people as part of implementation and use suggestions as part of the training.

Allow people to learn at their own pace; provide opportunities for hands-on experience; make training relevant to the job and have line managers project manage training.

Use different learning approaches; respect and use people's experience and allow people to solve problems and utilize their solutions.

Incorporate feedback into the training programme.

To build commitment to change (points 10–12)

- Does the change impose new controls on people, performances, costs, etc?
- Does the change reduce discretion?
- Are there incentives built into the change?

Plan change to bring benefits by using it to increase personal control over the job (and accountability); enhance people's jobs and status; ensure quick, visible benefits and provide incentives for people to go for change.

Involve people by asking for suggestions; specify milestones and ask for feedback and publicize ways in which suggestions and feedback are utilized.

To provide feedback to those involved (points 13–15)

- Do visible benefits occur?
- Is the impact on cost, performance, profit and resource utilization well documented?

Make sure that results are well documented, accessible, quickly available, positively described, relevant and ensure achievement of milestones is recognized.

Arrange wide recognition of success of people involved throughout the organization and specify how the change has helped the organization achieve its goals.

To manage the stress induced by change (points 16–18)

- Are people subject to high levels of stress?
- Is performance declining due to stress?
- Is there a higher incidence of 'people' problems?

Plan change to control the impact on people and seek ways of controlling the pressure. Allow more resources and time where the changes are novel. Adopt a rapid implementation plan where people have been consulted and agree to change. Empathize, constantly reinforce change, communicate and listen.

Money Matters plc – Implementing Change

From the implementation exercise one aspect of implementation at Money Matters plc that emerged as needing particular attention was the problem of resistance to change. Two management workshops were set up to consider the implementation of change at Money Matters. Thirty-two participants responded to points 1 to 3 of Checklist. Table 7.1 shows the results.

We know from the organizational assessment and from the table that the bank culture is risk-averse. The statements selected for these three points at Money Matters plc were predominantly the third or fourth options. Possible techniques for dealing with resistance to change and risk aversion are listed under Methods for Implementing Change. Therefore in developing an implementation plan for Money Matters plc we should consider ways of building into the plan:

- clear and accessible information for employees
- changes being sold realistically with benefits clearly described
- managers spending time diagnosing problems carefully
- changes started with pilot schemes
- pilot schemes introduced such that early success can be obtained.

Table 7.1	**Responses to points 1 to 3 in Checklist 1**			
1 In the past, new policies or systems introduced by the management have been:	Seen as meeting employees' needs	Not well understood	Greeted with some resistance	Vigorously resisted
	5%	18%	56%	21%
2 Employees may be best described as:	Innovative	Independent	Apathetic	Conservative or resistant to change
	0%	32%	45%	23%
3 The most recent and widely known change in the organization is viewed as:	A success	Moderately successful	Had no obvious impact	Not successful
	0%	15%	56%	29%

Change Management Skills

Gaining an understanding of an individual's change management skills provides a good basis for individual development. This exercise comprises a questionnaire on change management skills. These skills have been identified from research into a wide range of management jobs across a range of change management settings and situations.

Complete Part A of the questionnaire by rating the importance of the skill now and in the future (for example in five years' time) by using the five-point scale and circling the appropriate number. In some cases, therefore, you will have two ratings, for example:

1/1	identifies problems and			Now		Future
	causes systematically	1	2	③	4	⑤

You should complete one copy of the questionnaire, and ideally a second copy should be completed by your manager.

Complete Part B of the questionnaire by rating your own performance in terms of each skill listed. Please leave some time between completing Part A and Part B.

Change management skills, Part A

1 Not Important	2 Of some importance	3 Important but not essential	4 Definitely of importance	5 Of vital importance

1 Preparing for change

1.1	Identifies problems and causes systematically	1	2	3	4	5
1.2	Remains calm under pressure	1	2	3	4	5
1.3	Involves others when appropriate	1	2	3	4	5
1.4	Builds an open climate for decision making	1	2	3	4	5
1.5	Sets and agrees objectives	1	2	3	4	5
1.6	Draws out the input and contribution of others	1	2	3	4	5
1.7	Checks for agreement to proposals	1	2	3	4	5
1.8	Reviews objectives carefully	1	2	3	4	5
1.9	Seeks all information relevant to a decision	1	2	3	4	5
1.10	Is effective in presenting ideas and proposals	1	2	3	4	5

2 Planning changes

2.1	Identifies opportunities and solutions	1	2	3	4	5
2.2	Evaluates opportunities and solutions	1	2	3	4	5
2.3	Communicates information and views clearly	1	2	3	4	5
2.4	Generates imaginative solutions to problems	1	2	3	4	5
2.5	Identifies problems of implementation, resources required and appropriate priorities	1	2	3	4	5

3. Implementing changes

3.1	Identifies what needs to be done to achieve a plan for change	1	2	3	4	5
3.2	Achieves deadlines and meets appropriate priorities	1	2	3	4	5
3.3	Identifies impact of changes on people	1	2	3	4	5

Toolkit

3.4	Identifies and deals with impact of pressure/stress on self	1	2	3	4	5
3.5	Identifies and deals with impact of pressure/stress on others	1	2	3	4	5
3.6	Allocates tasks sensibly	1	2	3	4	5
3.7	Co-ordinates plans and actions effectively	1	2	3	4	5
4. Sustaining changes						
4.1	Makes the time to review progress and problems	1	2	3	4	5
4.2	Discusses problems and issues openly	1	2	3	4	5
4.3	Provides relevant positive feedback to people	1	2	3	4	5
4.4	Identifies areas for improvement	1	2	3	4	5
4.5	Builds well on success, keeping motivation high	1	2	3	4	5
4.6	Builds team spirit	1	2	3	4	5
4.7	Sets out to increase the use of resources	1	2	3	4	5
4.8	Allows enough time for change	1	2	3	4	5

Change management skills, Part B

Toolkit

1 Inadequate	2 Poor	3 Average	4 Very Good		5 Excellent				
1 Preparing for change									
1.1	Identifies problems and causes systematically			1	2	3	4	5	
1.2	Remains calm under pressure			1	2	3	4	5	
1.3	Involves others when appropriate			1	2	3	4	5	
1.4	Builds an open climate for decision making			1	2	3	4	5	
1.5	Sets and agrees objectives			1	2	3	4	5	
1.6	Draws out the input and contribution of others			1	2	3	4	5	
1.7	Checks for agreement to proposals			1	2	3	4	5	
1.8	Reviews objectives carefully			1	2	3	4	5	

| 1.9 | Seeks all information relevant to a decision | 1 | 2 | 3 | 4 | 5 |
| 1.10 | Is effective in presenting ideas and proposals | 1 | 2 | 3 | 4 | 5 |

2 Planning changes

2.1	Identifies opportunities and solutions	1	2	3	4	5
2.2	Evaluates opportunities and solutions	1	2	3	4	5
2.3	Communicates information and views clearly	1	2	3	4	5
2.4	Generates imaginative solutions to problems	1	2	3	4	5
2.5	Identifies problems of implementation, resources required and appropriate priorities	1	2	3	4	5

3. Implementing changes

3.1	Identifies what needs to be done to achieve a plan for change	1	2	3	4	5
3.2	Achieves deadlines and meets appropriate priorities	1	2	3	4	5
3.3	Identifies impact of changes on people	1	2	3	4	5
3.4	Identifies and deals with impact of pressure/stress on self	1	2	3	4	5
3.5	Identifies and deals with impact of pressure/stress on others	1	2	3	4	5
3.6	Allocates tasks sensibly	1	2	3	4	5
3.7	Co-ordinates plans and actions effectively	1	2	3	4	5

4. Sustaining changes

4.1	Makes the time to review progress and problems	1	2	3	4	5
4.2	Discusses problems and issues openly	1	2	3	4	5
4.3	Provides relevant positive feedback to people	1	2	3	4	5
4.4	Identifies areas for improvement	1	2	3	4	5
4.5	Builds well on success, keeping motivation high	1	2	3	4	5
4.6	Builds team spirit	1	2	3	4	5
4.7	Sets out to increase the use of resources	1	2	3	4	5
4.8	Allows enough time for change	1	2	3	4	5

Change management skills, Analysis

Toolkit

	Part A Importance now	Part A Future Importance	Part B Performance
1.1			
1.2			
1.3			
1.4			
1.5			
1.6			
1.7			
1.8			
1.9			
1.10			
2.1			
2.2			
2.3			
2.4			
2.5			
3.1			
3.2			
3.3			
3.4			
3.5			
3.6			
3.7			
4.1			
4.2			
4.3			
4.4			
4.5			
4.6			
4.7			
4.8			

If both you and your manager have completed the questionnaires you can now identify your strengths, skills development needs and change management development needs.

- **strengths** – those rated 4 or 5 on your performance by both you and your manager.
- **skills development needs** – those rated important *now* – 3, 4 or 5 – by you *and* your manager, but where your performance is inadequate – 2 or 1 – as rated by you *or* your manager.
- **development needs** – those rated by your manager as likely to be important – 4 or 5 – in 3 to 5 years' time but where your performance is inadequate – 2 or 1 – as rated by you *or* your manager.

Toolkit

Strengths

a

b

c

d

e

Skills development needs

a

b

c

d

e

Action (list possible actions to meet skills development needs)

a

b

c

d

e

Change management development needs

a

b

Toolkit

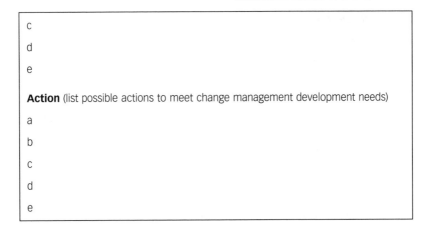

c

d

e

Action (list possible actions to meet change management development needs)

a

b

c

d

e

Money Matters plc – Change Management Skills

From this exercise the key weakness identified for Money Matters plc was in the area of feedback-sustaining change. The feedback processes were too formal, too structured and one way. One of the changes included in the implementation plan was to design a more open and problem-oriented approach to performance review meetings. The present approach tended to leave managers, particularly branch managers, feeling very defensive about performance issues. This militated against open discussions of problems and reinforced the risk-averse culture. Drawing these managers into the discussion of 'group' problems at review meetings is one way of working with this weakness by changing the way the review meetings are handled. In consequence the manager running the performance review meeting needs to develop higher level presentation skills, team building skills and feedback skills. These are skills development needs.

Possible actions to meet these needs include attending a presentation skills course, and restructuring the performance review meetings by interspersing shorter presentations with problem solving sessions where groups of managers work on problems identified in the presentation. The presentation skills course will improve the skills level, shorter presentations are likely to be more focused and draw a better audience response, and problem solving involves people, builds teams and presents opportunities for feedback.

A change management development need identified was that of motivating the sales force. Managers in the group understood how to motivate branch staff but not sales staff. This is a major development area for managers.

Assessing Change Risk

This tool looks systematically at change risk.

You should access commitment to change by looking at the six factors in Figure 7.1 relevant to this dimension. Clearly the higher each is then the higher will be commitment. Thus the linkage is marked with +.

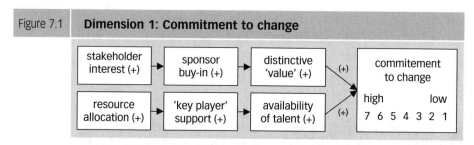

Figure 7.1 — **Dimension 1: Commitment to change**

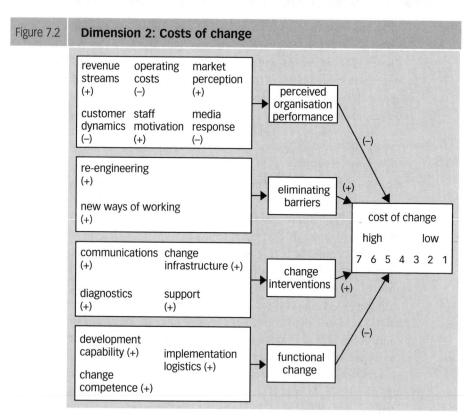

Figure 7.2 — **Dimension 2: Costs of change**

Again look at each box in Figure 7.2 in developing an overall view about the cost of change. In some cases the factor is to be assessed as either simple or complex, i.e. customer dynamics or likely pattern of buying behaviour. By 'complex' we mean difficult and therefore expensive to predict. In this case the linkages are both positive and negative, i.e. the higher the perceived organization performance, the lower the cost of change ultimately, but the more extensive the effort will be to remove barriers to change or the scope of change interventions and the higher the cost of change. Thus you will need to make a judgement as to how the various factors will balance out.

Transition stability represent an assessment of how 'bumpy' the change process may be (Figure 7.3). Are there inherent problems in implementing the changes involved? These might be internal or external. In practice the judgement here is on the question: 'Are the likely benefits worth the pain and disruption?'

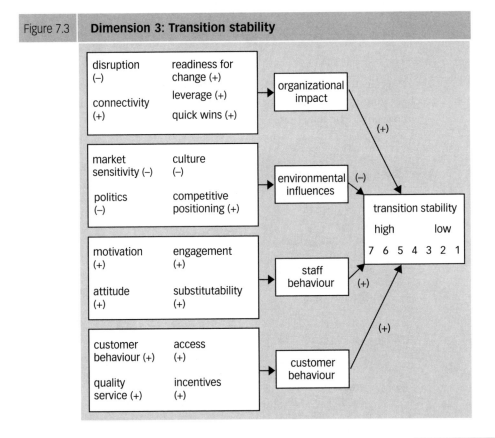

Figure 7.3   Dimension 3: Transition stability

Figure 7.4	**Dimension 4: Sustained performance**

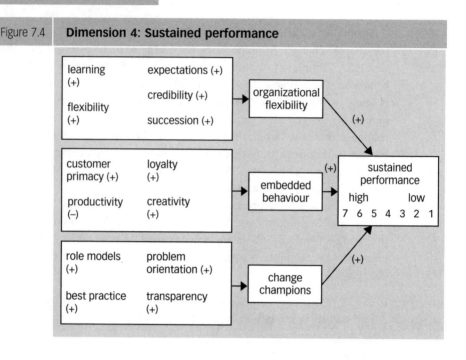

Sustained performance refers to whether changes can be 'embedded' and have long-term impact. Here we look at whether the changes really will have impact over the long-run.

Figure 7.5	**Scoring change risk**

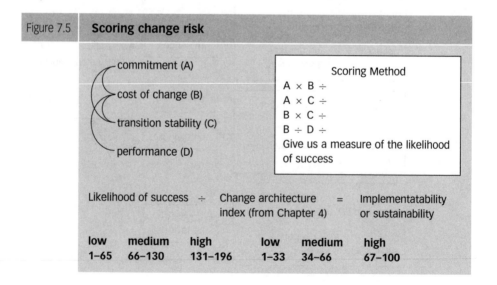

Scoring system

The four dimensions interact. To keep the analysis reasonably simple we identify the key interactions in Figure 7.5 and then show the scoring method.

Here the concern is to judge whether or not the proposed changes will be embedded such that the expected gains will be achieved.

Final Comment

You should not become too focused on the numbers. The main purpose of the exercise was to get you to think through change risk, success and sustainability. This is the key issue for change – can we make it sustainable? Many of the factors will not apply, if so ignore them. Remember this is a learning process about your change, not a framework to tell you how to think. So stay in control and use it sensibly!

In this chapter we looked at implementation, your own change management skills and at change risk. This ought to have helped you identify the gaps that you need to fill in order to enhance the likelihood of success in change management. You can then think through how to fill those gaps in conjunction with the change architecture technique noting that integration is the key to maximizing the leverage of any particular change programme.

In this toolkit we have sought to help you understand how to identify what needs to change and how to go about changing it. The author is continually conducting researching on how organizations go about change management and what leads to success in change. Should you wish to contact him you can do so on colin.carnall@henleymc.ac.uk.

References

Alexander, L.D. (1985) 'Successfully Implementing Strategic Decisions', *Long Range Planning*, **18** (3), 91–97.

Ansoff, I. and McDonnell, E. (1985) *Implanting Strategic Management*, New York: Prentice Hall.

Argyris, C. (1990) *Overcoming Organizational Defences*, Needham Heights: Allyn and Bacon.

Beckhard, R. and Pritchard, W. (1992) *Changing the Essence*, San Francisco: Jossey-Bass.

Boonstra, J. (2002) *The Psychological Management of Organisational Change*, Chichester: J. Wiley & Sons.

Bruch, H. and Sattelberger, T. (2001) 'The turnaround at Lufthansa', *Journal of Change Management*, **1** (4), 344–365.

Bunker, B.B. and Alban, B.T. (1996) *Large Group Interventions: Engaging the Whole System for Rapid Change*, San Francisco: Jossey-Bass.

Burke, W.W. and Litwin, G.H. (1992) 'A Causal Model of Organizational Performance and Change', *Journal of Management*, **18** (3), 528.

Carnall, C.A. (2002) 'Change Architecture', in J. Boonstra (ed), *The Psychological Management of Organization Change*, London: John Wiley & Sons.

Carnall, C.A. (1982) *The Evaluation of Work Organization Change*, Farnborough: Gower.

Clark, J. (1995) *Managing Innovation and Change*, London: Sage.

Clark, K.B. and Fujimoto, T. (1991) *Product Development Performance*, Boston: Harvard Business School Press.

Cope, M. (1996) 'The use of stage events to mobilise change', paper presented at the Academy of Human Resource Development, Henley Management College, Henley-on-Thames, 28 July 1996.

Deal, T.E. and Kennedy, A. (1982) *Corporate Cultures*, Reading, MA: Addison-Wesley.

Edmonson, A., Bohmer, R. and Pisaro, G. (2001) 'Speeding up team learning', *Harvard Business Review*, **79** (9) 125–134.

Ellinor, L. and Gerard, G. (1998) *Dialogue*, New York: John Wiley & Sons.

Emery, M. and Purser, R.E. (1996) *The Search Conference*, San Francisco: Jossey Bass.

Felix, E. (2000) 'Creating radical change: producer choice at the BBC', *Journal of Change Management*, **1** (1), 5–21.

Fukuyama, F. (1995) *Trust: The Social Virtues and the Creation of Prosperity*, London: Hamish Hamilton.

Gilbert, X. and Strebel, P. (1989) 'From innovation to outpacing', *Business Quarterly*, (Summer), 19–22.

Goffee, R. and Jones, G. (1998) *The Character of the Corporation*, New York: Harper Business.

Gratton, L. (2000) *Living Strategy*, Harlow, Essex: Prentice Hall.

Grünig, R. and Kühn, R. (2001) *Process-based Strategic Planning*, Berlin: Springer.

Hampden-Turner, C. (1990) *Charting the Corporate Mind*, London: Basic Blackwell.

Handy, C. (1976) *Understanding Organisations*, Harmondsworth: Penguin.

Harrison, R. (1970) *What Kind of Organisation?* London: Development Research Associates.

Higgs, M. and Rowland, D. (2000) 'Building Change Leadership Capability: The Quest for Change Competance', *Journal of Change Management*, 1 (2), 116–131.

Higgs, M. and Rowland, D. (2001) 'Developing change leaders', *Journal of Change Management*, **2** (1), 47–66.

Hofstede, G. (1988) *Cultures Consequences*, Harmondsworth: Penguin.

Jacobs, R.W. (1994) *Real Time Strategic Change*, San Francisco: Berrett-Koehler.

Kaplan, R.S. and Norton, D.P. (1996*) The Balanced Scorecard: Turning Strategy into Action*, Boston: Harvard Business School Press.

Kay, J. (1993) *Foundations of Corporate Success*, Oxford: Oxford University Press.

Manzoni, M. (2000) Paper presented to E-HR 2000 Conference, London, 25–28 September 2000.

Markides, C. (2000) *All the Right Moves: A Guide to Crafting Breakthrough Strategy*, Boston: Harvard Business School Press.

Martin, J. (1995) *The Great Transition*, New York: American Management Association.

McGrath, R.G. and MacMillan, I.C. (2000) *The Entrepreneurial Mindset*, Boston: Harvard Business School Press.

Meyerson, D.E. (2001) 'Radical change, the quiet way', *Harvard Business Review*, **79** (9), 92–104.

Munch, B. (2001) 'Changing a culture of face time', *Harvard Business Review*, **79** (10), 125–132.

Neumann, J.E., Holti, R. and Standing, H. (1995) *Changing Everything at Once*, London: Tavistock Institute.

Norlton, G. (1998) 'Creating an opportunity for positive change', MBA dissertation, Henley Management College, Henley-on-Thames.

Ohmae, H. (1987) *Mobilizing Invisible Assets*, Cambridge: Harvard University Press.

Pfeffer, J. (1998) *The Human Equation*, Boston: Harvard Business School Press.

Porter, M. (1985) *Competitive Advantage*, New York: Free Press.

Pressman, J.L. and Wildavsky, A. (1973) *Implementation*, Los Angeles: University of California Press.

Quinn, J.B. (1992) *The Intelligent Enterprise*, New York: Free Press.

Quinn Mills, D. (1991) *The Cluster Organization*, New York: John Wiley & Sons.

Rubinstein, M.F., and Firstenberg, I.R. (1999) *The Minding Organization*, New York: John Wiley & Sons.

Schein, F. (1992) *Organization Culture and Leadership*, San Francisco: Jossey-Bass.

Stalk, G and Hout, J.M. (1990) *Competing Against Time*, New York: Free Press.

Thornbury, J. (1999) 'KPMG; Revitalising culture through values', *Business Strategy Review*, **10** (4), 1–15.

Tichy, N. and Sherman, S. (1995) *Control Your Destiny*, London: Harper Collins.

Vince, R. (1996) *Managing Change*, Bristol: Policy Press.

Index